YOUR SHERPA
YOUR PARENTAL GUIDE TO FINANCIAL LITERACY

Helping Parents Help Their Kids, in Three Parts:

You Can't Begin to Save if You Have Too Much Student Debt,
You Can't Save if You Can't Get and Hold a Good Job, and
Making Daily Decisions to Save and Build Wealth

JEFF TYBURSKI

AUTHORS PLACE
— PRESS —

Published by Authors Place Press
9885 Wyecliff Drive, Suite 200
Highlands Ranch, CO 80126
Authorsplace.com

Manufactured in the United States of America.

ISBN: 978-1-62865-677-0

This book conveys the teaching content of Your Sherpa, LLC, which offers financial literacy educational services with the focus on teaching people how to save money. Your Sherpa, LLC does not provide investment advice, is not a financial advisor or dealer-broker, and does not discuss specific securities.

CONTENTS

DEDICATION

For my mother-in-law, Beth Frind, who introduced me to personal finance, the financial markets, and a lifestyle of daily decisions to save and build wealth.

In the early 1990s Beth taped a weekend radio show called *Bob Brinker's Moneytalk©*, meticulously paused the recording during commercials, and gave me the cassettes for my commute.

Thanks for being the spark. We miss you, Beth.

A WORD FROM THE AUTHOR

Let's work together to set your children up for success! This book shows you what we can teach your children about saving money and the obstacles preventing people from saving (e.g., excessive student debt). Along the way, as a parent, you too can learn and benefit financially. If you can convince your child to read along, great. If not, know that **this book is part of a broader platform, including audio lessons and other online resources, specifically designed to connect with a younger audience** (see www.**your**financial**sherpa**.com).

Let's work together to get in front of and avoid some serious problems! High school and college students make major life decisions. They select their career objectives, choose a college, and set out to earn and handle money. These are decisions and activities with huge financial implications. However, many students and families are unprepared and are making poor decisions with long-lasting ill effects. For instance, a degree that saddles the student and parent with crippling debt, but doesn't help the graduate get a good job, is right for no one! I will give you a road map and personal process to avoid such an outcome.

This is not a sci-fi thriller. To your credit, you have cracked open an educational book. But relax, I've worked hard to make this book easy to understand, engaging, and not about math. **Key tenants of my teaching approach are that I aim to challenge conventional wisdom and to deliver epiphany moments, sudden bursts of insight that change you in some way.**

I offer a refreshingly frank conversation about the challenges people face to save money, the broken systems that perpetuate these problems, and how it is our individual responsibility, starting at a surprisingly young age, to overcome these headwinds.

These were my goals when I set out to write a book:

1. **Create a framework people can remember and apply to their daily lives.**

2. **Improve some lives.**

3. **Inspire people to want to explore and learn more.**

4. **Keep it short!**

Parents: As you read this book, imagine sitting in the back of a classroom listening to a message I am delivering to your children. This book primarily speaks to the student (e.g., "pursue your passions", "you can't begin to save if you have too much debt", "you can't save if you can't get and hold a good job").

INTRODUCTION

YOUR SHERPA

"It's not a hill, it's a mountain - as you start out the climb."

U2

A sherpa provides expert guidance on Himalayan climbs. A sherpa prepares, teaches, and supports the climber before and along the journey. I, too, try to guide people as a *financial sherpa*. When people hear the word financial, they tend to think of investing and the financial markets. Many investment firms have names that evoke an image of the peak, summit, or pinnacle, symbolizing the end point (i.e., retirement). In contrast, **my concern,** and why I started teaching financial literacy, **is that too few people are saving money in the first place.** You need to save (i.e., put money aside for the future), before you can invest (i.e., put some savings to work to grow). So, **for people, especially young people, who need help learning how to save money, I, as *Your Sherpa*, am with you at the beginning, at base camp.** *Base camp* is where there is a need to learn the basics, to receive inspiration and guidance, and is the place from where you set out on the journey to achieve your financial goals.

My base camp analogy falls short in one important respect. Those who show up at Mount Everest's base camp are there by choice. They need to learn more about climbing at that elevation, and they need guidance on the specific route, but they *love* to climb. With financial literacy, even though people of all ages can learn and benefit, most people don't seek out help or even have the awareness that they need help. *Few people have an explicit passion for financial literacy.*

To overcome this challenge, I plan to demonstrate that **financial literacy is a means to an end, a tool for better lifestyle choices and outcomes.** Financial literacy may at times involve numbers and math, but it is mostly about a mind set and life choice. Learning to become financially literate doesn't have to feel like a tedious academic exercise. In fact, it can be quite exciting to go counter to the crowd and conventional thinking – to live modestly in a consumer-driven economy and to pursue a *career* you love in a time when many go deep into college debt assuming the *degree* is the be all and end all. It can be empowering and exhilarating to both enjoy life today while saving for and planning for your future. Like a snowball rolling downhill, growing and gaining momentum, your increasing knowledge and sense of urgency can motivate you further and those around you will benefit.

Financial Literacy Reflected in Lifestyle Choices and Outcomes:

Let's look at this view of financial literacy from four perspectives: one's approach to life, money, college, and career. Maybe you can personally relate with some of these tendencies.

- **Approach to life:** Those who are financially literate think long-term. Many people have dreams, but those who are financially literate set specific goals and make plans to achieve them. They enjoy life today but relish in the opportunity to prepare for an even better tomorrow. They have a personal process to make daily decisions to save and build wealth. For instance, they make saving a priority by participating in an employer-sponsored pre-tax savings plan. They make sound financial decisions when it comes to their housing, transportation, and even routine purchases. They avoid obstacles, like excessive debt, that can derail their plans and are better prepared for an emergency. *Those who are not financially literate* often live purely in the moment. They think responsibilities in the future can be tackled when they present themselves.

- **Approach to money:** Those who are financially literate tend to see money as a tool or means to achieve dreams. They put money to work for them, to grow. They are genuinely excited about the power of compounding and the fact that money can make more money. They also "get it", that compounding is not just a bonus or luxury, that the list of future needs is so long that most of us are unable to simply set aside enough for future needs. We *need* compounding to provide the necessary growth. With diverse investments and insurance, those who are financially literate are prepared for future financial needs, to care for their children, and to give to others. *Those who are not financially literate* tend to work for their money but see little reward as they live paycheck to paycheck (even if their pay increases), or they routinely go beyond what they earn and take on debt.

- **Approach to college:** For those who are financially literate their top priority is to get a job and career. College may not even be necessary for their dreams. If it is, their main goal is to get the degree they need with minimal debt. They may even be open to creative approaches like attending a community college for the first two years, to save money. They only visit, and eventually choose, a school they can truly afford. *Those who are not financially literate* often fall in love with a campus or school name and make a largely emotional decision. They fail to see the double whammy of college debt, that you must pay debt back with interest and it is a lost opportunity to save at a young age when the time value of money is greatest.

- **Approach to a career:** Those who are financially literate recognize that it is their responsibility to proactively stay employable in today's world of career uncertainty. They embrace change and invest in themselves. With their personal process they tend to have a healthier work/life balance. *Those who are not financially literate* may not be prepared to stay employed or to grow their income.

As you can see, lifestyle choices, particularly financial choices, can impact outcomes.

ACTIVITY - FINANCIAL LITERACY, WHAT IS AT STAKE?

Let's **quantify what is at stake** as we begin to think about saving and building wealth.

My goal for this activity is to **illustrate the power of money compounding and working for you. This will illustrate the benefit of starting to save when young**.

The situation is as follows: We have two people. Each saves $100 per month for 10 years. Thus, each saves the same amount, $12,000. One saves in his/her 20s. The other saves in his/her 40s. The money saved is invested and compounds at 7% per year until age 60 producing a different final balance for each person.

Without performing or worrying about the underlying calculations, what do you think best describes the difference in final balances at age 60?

a. within $10,000 of each other

b. the higher amount is about 2x the lower

c. the higher amount is about 4x the lower

Well, the correct answer is c! The person who started saving, and putting that savings to work, in their 20s, under our assumptions, will end up with more than 4x the person who started saving in their 40s! That is, the person who saved in their 20s saw their $12,000 grow to over $126,000. However, the person who saved the same amount, but not until their 40s, saw that grow to only $32,000.

One more point to close out our activity: not only does the person who saved at a younger age have approximately 4x the person who saved later in life, but also note that they have over 10x what they originally saved! **There are significant benefits to giving your money more time to grow. Hopefully, seeing this example motivates you to want to learn more about saving and building wealth.**

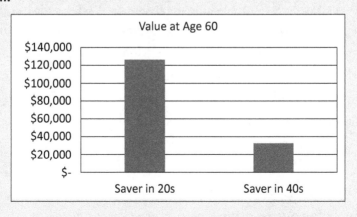

Welcome to Base Camp - Orientation Remarks:

At a high level, **helping people achieve their financial goals is my ultimate mission**. I believe there is a life-changing progression or **virtuous cycle** that flows from achieving financial goals. If you achieve financial goals, you tend to be able to take more control of your life and the path you are on. If you have more control, you are best positioned to unlock your personal potential.

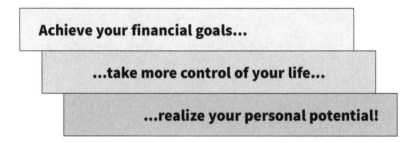

Unlocking and realizing your personal potential sounds rather lofty, but maybe we can agree to at least try to pursue the first hurdle, achieving your financial goals.

Achieving financial goals, which begins with a focus on saving, is surely easier said than done. To attend a private college today, it costs about $35,000 per year, with many schools as high as $50,000-$80,000 per year. Seriously, I said that right. Even state schools may cost $25,000-35,000 per year[1]. Multiply the per year cost to attend college times the number of years to graduate, which on average now is closer to five than four, to arrive at the cost to get a degree. Multiply the cost to get a degree times the number of children in a family going to college, and you arrive at a sum that is hard to fathom and only addresses a family's need to save for college. We must save for retirement as well, at a time now when only about 13% of workers will receive a pension[2]. All along, we must support our daily expenses and likely save for a home too.

As you can see, **we have a lot of financial responsibility these days to provide for our own futures!** And **yet**, despite how daunting these numbers are, according to surveys by the Federal Reserve Board and CareerBuilder respectively:

- **About 40% of Americans say they can't raise even $400 for an emergency.**[3]
- **More than 75% of American households live paycheck to paycheck.**[4] It's counterintuitive, but even as families earn more, they often continue to live paycheck to paycheck. They simply spend more instead of saving.

My prior observation about unlocking your potential if you achieve financial goals was not a synonym for *money buys you happiness* because even a big pile of money can disappear with poor decisions. Just search the long list of celebrities and professional athletes who made millions and now have nothing!

There is a large gap between what is needed to achieve financial goals and what some people are doing with their money and spending choices.

I said my broad mission is to help you achieve financial goals because that allows you to take more control of your life and increases the chances that you really unlock your full potential. To begin to develop a specific road map for you, I need to break that broad mission into achievable milestones.

Why I Started Teaching Financial Literacy – The Problems

I see three serious problems acting as headwinds preventing people from even setting out to achieve their financial goals. Most people, especially young people, are unprepared to meet these challenges. These problems are:

- **Soaring college debt** - *Many people can't begin to save and build wealth because they are deep in a financial hole due to crippling debt.* College debt is the prime culprit and my focus. As we'll discuss, I think the college selection process is a broken system, essentially resulting in students and families making emotional, not sound financial, decisions. College is expensive. I don't expect that to change. But that fact alone shouldn't mean that students and families choose schools they can't afford. College debt is creating both a millennial and parental financial crisis. There is a millennial financial crisis occurring as young people aren't saving money at an early age, precisely when you want to be doing so to benefit from the power of compounding interest. Too many people entering the workforce today can't save because they are starting in a college debt-driven hole. There is a parental financial crisis too. With good intentions, parents are mortgaging their own futures and trashing their retirement plans to put kids through college.

- **Career uncertainty** - *People can't save because they can't get and hold a good job or grow their income.* Teaching people how to save money can focus too narrowly on controlling spending. Growing your earning power also shapes your ability to provide for your future. However, due to a host of factors including technological change and globalization, people today are very unsure about their potential to earn a higher income. In fact, today there is broad uncertainty about even getting and holding a good job. This problem builds on the first. The assumption that a degree alone guarantees a successful career is flawed.

- **A general lack of financial literacy** - *Even if people avoid college debt and get a good job, many simply do NOT know how to save.* Alarmingly, this is occurring just as the need to be financially literate is rising, because it is increasingly our responsibility to save money and fund our financial futures. Parents also suffer from a general inability to teach their kids about money, as many are not financially literate themselves.

Why I Started Teaching Financial Literacy – My Mission

The three problems that catalyzed me into action are **serious problems**. The root causes are not going away. I want students, parents, and families to **be aware of and ahead of them with a *personal process* to stay out of trouble.** I have a specific mission for each problem:

The Problems	My Mission
Soaring college debt	Prevent
Career uncertainty	Adapt
Lack of financial literacy	Solve

- **Soaring college debt** – My mission is to help you attain the career you want with minimal debt.

- **Career uncertainty** – My mission is to teach you how to adapt and proactively stay employable in our ever-changing world.

- **A general lack of financial literacy** - My mission is to teach you why we must save, how to save, and what to do with savings.

As you can see, my focus is on the need to save money and to remove or avoid the obstacles preventing people from saving.

How I Differentiate

I have a differentiated, effective approach to teaching financial literacy. A look across the landscape of resources for personal finance education identifies many websites, online tools, and *apps*. Much of this content focuses on math and underlying methodology. Math and methods are important, but **I am more about a qualitative approach and delivering epiphany moments that act as sudden bursts of inspiration and insight. I deliver epiphanies that help you realize that saving money is important and that you can do it; revelations that you *need* to do this** like a climber *needs* a final push to the summit.

My unique approach to teaching financial literacy is reflected in how I **view** financial literacy and the **scope** of my content:

- **View:** I view financial literacy as a **lifelong process requiring *daily* decisions to save and sustainable lifestyle choices**. I take a *life cycle* approach, teaching students, young adults, adults, and parents.

Life Cycle Approach to My Teaching Content					
	Student			Adult	
	Middle School	High School	College	Working	Parent
Main Message	Spark interest: money can grow!	Avoid or minimize debt. Get a career, not just a degree. Is college right for you, or necessary for your goals?		Learn why we must save and how to save, and how to grow your earnings!	Teach your kids and minimize your own college debt.

- **Scope:** While in one respect I narrowly focus on teaching people to save, I also broaden the scope to address obstacles preventing people from saving. Career choice, the cost of the college you select, and how you stay employable throughout your career have huge financial implications. I see these topics as a natural fit and necessity in a financial literacy curriculum.

What I Do – Key Principles Framework

We've covered WHY I started, referring to the problems I see and my mission with respect to them, and HOW I am different. Now let's see more specifically WHAT I do. **All of my teaching content, and the rest of this book, uses the framework shown below.** You will see this graphic over and over again serving as a *signpost*, reminding you of your current location within the broader framework.

There are the three problems that motivated me into action: the soaring levels of college debt, career uncertainty, and the general lack of financial literacy. I tackle one problem at a time and break the solution into digestible parts with **individual chapters literally built around, and aimed at delivering, epiphanies**. I also describe some *broken systems* around you, not to shift blame but to inform you. I will keep the focus on you and how **it is *your* responsibility** to cope with, and adjust to, your environment.

Framework:

Problem	Solution	Epiphany
Soaring college debt	Get a career, not just a degree, with minimal debt	A *broken* system
		Career goals - Pursue your passions
		Estimate your earning potential
		Choose a school you can afford
Career uncertainty	Proactively stay employable	Career uncertainty *will* affect you
		Adopt a mindset that embraces change
		Keep investing in yourself
Lack of financial literacy	Learn **why** we *must* save	You *need* compounding
	Learn **how** to save	*You* control your mindset
		Save *first*
		Live for *today* - "What's your butter?"
	Learn **what** to do with savings	It's *not* too intimidating

Next - We dive into the three problems preventing most people from achieving financial goals:

The Problems	Section of Book
Soaring college debt	You Can't Begin to **Save** if You Have Too Much Student Debt
Career uncertainty	You Can't **Save** if You Can't Get and Hold a Good Job
Lack of financial literacy	Making Daily Decisions to **Save** and Build Wealth

PART I

YOU CAN'T BEGIN TO SAVE IF YOU HAVE TOO MUCH STUDENT DEBT

"We keep lending money we don't have to people who can't pay it back for jobs that don't exist."

Mike Rowe, on college debt and blindly pursuing college degrees

Part I fit in overall framework:

Problem	Solution	Epiphany
Soaring college debt	Get a career, not just a degree, with minimal debt	A *broken* system
		Career goals - Pursue your passions
		Estimate your earning potential
		Choose a school you can afford
Career uncertainty	Proactively stay employable	Career uncertainty *will* affect you
		Adopt a mindset that embraces change
		Keep investing in yourself
Lack of financial literacy	Learn **why** we *must* save	You *need* compounding
	Learn **how** to save	*You* control your mindset
		Save *first*
		Live for *today* - "What's your butter?"
	Learn **what** to do with savings	It's *not* too intimidating

This book is about saving money and building wealth. Unfortunately, you can't begin to save if you have too much debt. Part I addresses soaring college loan debt and offers alternative strategies to students and parents.

The process to choose a college is intimidating, if not totally overwhelming. I've been there with my kids. The cost to attend many schools literally seems hard to comprehend or justify, and the price that applies to you doesn't seem transparent. Plus, the whole *system* and national narrative is built entirely on a flawed assumption that everyone should go to college in the first place.

In an ideal world, the goal of this section would be to help students and parents *totally avoid* college debt. Given the high and rising costs of attending college, which we cannot change, **a more realistic goal is to help you *minimize* debt.** I also openly encourage you to consider options other than college.

Despite the daunting cost of college, I see and hear of behavior as if people aren't even looking at the numbers. It's hardly a joking matter but have you heard any of these, or similar, anecdotes? They are somewhat comical in a sad way.

- The student who became fixated on an $80,000 per year college because the club volleyball coach sent her a personal email wanting her to be on the team.

- The students who only consider schools with recognizable names from the NCAA basketball tournament.

- The students who think it is beneath them to go to a community college, trade school, or apprenticeship program. This is probably not a surprise with the national narrative calling these *alternatives*. This despite millions of job openings in our country which don't require four-year degrees and millions of college graduates unemployed or not using their very expensive degrees.

- The countless high school students who visit schools and even make a final choice without even knowing the full costs to attend or the impact both on their future finances and their parents' retirement plans.

- The students who, despite the high cost of attendance, push ahead to go to college with no specific career objectives, selected major, or any hope of graduating on time in four years.

- The students and families who receive a letter describing their financial aid package, but they don't really understand how to read it or how much of it represents loans which must be paid back with interest.

- The parents and students who don't openly talk about how much the family has saved *for college* and what would really be an affordable school for them.

- The students who add the costs of spring break to their student loan balances.

- And of course, the illegal shenanigans of the 2019 admissions scandal.

We've all had delicate, uncomfortable, or even painful conversations with our kids about their diets, exercise, electronic devices, social media, alcohol, sex, etc. Sometimes we throw up our hands, walk away, and hope for the best. Is college one of those times? **Do we defer to a 17-year-old, who we love dearly but likely wouldn't completely trust with a grocery list, a decision that may cost the family a quarter of a million dollars? Or do we apply a process to make the best decisions when we help them choose a career and select a college?**

Some college debt may be unavoidable. Some college debt is even reasonable and justified by the probability of higher future earning power. Of course, **a degree alone does not guarantee you higher income potential (nor does a degree from *certain* schools over others). As with all things in life, your future success will come down to you**: some combination of the effort, drive, and passion you put into your work and an element of luck. There are also plenty of examples of people who demonstrated competence in a field, combined with intense passion, and they succeeded *without* a college degree. If you do pursue a college degree, I want you to apply my framework to avoid joining the ranks of those taking on crippling amounts of debt.

By the end of this section you will be able to:

1. **Identify why so many students and parents borrow excessive amounts of college debt.** We will review the college selection process that students and families use when they choose a school. You will get to know the players affecting this decision, their roles, and how, unfortunately, despite good intentions, in the end, students often simply make emotional decisions to attend a school they really can't afford. I will point out problems, such as high costs of attendance and factors that perpetuate higher costs, but in the end will remind you that the final decision about which school to attend is *your* responsibility! I wish college cost less, but it doesn't work to blame the schools for charging what they can get, and we can't expect the system to change. We must find a way to succeed in this flawed environment.

2. **Develop a personal plan to get the degree you want while minimizing debt.** I encourage you to focus on the real end goal, getting a job and career, not just a degree. I encourage you to pursue your passions when you select your career goals and provide a framework to help you with that effort. *I also want you to honestly assess if college is right for you.* If you do pursue a college degree, I urge you to work very hard to graduate on time and progress towards employment in your selected field since the very high cost of college today demands a serious commitment. Above all, from a personal finance perspective, I want you to be positioned to pay back any debt you do assume.

This will also be the flow of this section: first the problem, then the solution. **My solution aims to provide a process to help you take the emotion out of the high stakes decision of choosing a school.**

INSIGHT - COLLEGE DEBT IS A *DOUBLE WHAMMY*

I want to show you that debt is both a hole you must dig out of and a lost opportunity to save money.

Let's analyze a $10,000 *chunk* of debt: What does it cost to pay off this amount? What are the benefits if you avoid this much debt?

First, remember debt is paid back with interest. That is, if you borrow $10,000, you pay back more than $10,000. Think of it as *the cost* of borrowing money. Prevailing conditions, for Parent PLUS loans, indicate that for every $10,000 in college debt you must pay back about $4,000 in interest, typically done over 10 years. So, **the first benefit of taking out less debt is paying less interest**. Avoid $10,000 in debt and **you avoid paying $4,000 in interest!**

What if, instead of paying your way out of a hole, you save and build wealth? You just saw that you'd save $4,000 in interest payments for every $10,000 in college debt you avoid. Far more significant, and what some people ignore or forget, is the opportunity cost (i.e., what you could otherwise be doing if you weren't paying back debt).

The monthly payment, under current conditions, to pay off $10,000 in debt is approximately $120/month for 10 years. If, instead of paying off debt, you paid yourself and saved the $120/month for 10 years and earned a reasonable investment return until you were age 60, **you would amass over $100,000 – yes, 10x $10,000!**

What is at stake if you avoid debt? ... the chance to build wealth!

As you can see, I want you to have a clear understanding of the impact of student debt. For mathematical simplicity, the above activity worked with a round number of $10,000 of debt, but the average student in America borrows over $30,000 to attend college. Many students and parents take on over $100,000 in debt. The above analysis showed you that **student debt is a *double whammy.*** Debt is both a hole you must dig out of and a missed opportunity to save, especially at a young age when the power of compounding is strongest.

INSIGHT – *FREE* COLLEGE

As we conclude this introduction to our discussion on choosing a college and college debt, you might be curious about my thoughts on the efforts and opinions to promote *free* college. The cynic in me will quickly say, "Nothing is free", but that is likely a flippant and dismissive response. More seriously, I can think of several potential negative outcomes associated with these proposals:

- **College is not right for everyone -** I already have a concern that college is not right for everyone, but we live in a country encouraging everyone to go. If the chorus gets louder about everyone going, for *free*, I worry that even more students, who actually have other passions and skills, will get degrees that don't suit them and debt they can't pay off. Yes, even *free* will result in debt since *free* likely only applies to tuition and not costly room and board.

- **Commoditization of the undergraduate degree -** I have an additional concern that too many and too easily attained undergraduate degrees will lessen their market value. This will simply lead to graduate degrees being required in more fields so job candidates can separate themselves. While a student may save some money at the undergraduate level, they will be forced to spend or borrow for graduate school while postponing their earnings years.

- **Diverts attention from how expensive college is -** I think college is unjustifiably expensive. I don't necessarily blame schools for that. They are charging what they can get. I am, however, discouraged by how rarely the high cost is seen as a problem. The focus is mostly on availability of loans. I think *free* school will continue to mask the underlying issues with cost. *Free* will only apply to some while others will have to contend with the full price.

Next – My hope is that my goal becomes your goal: for you to get the career and degree you need with minimal debt. It is your responsibility to make the right decisions that best position you to succeed going forward. The next three chapters will give you a framework and the necessary tools to accomplish this.

CHAPTER ONE

DEFINE THE PROBLEM – A BROKEN SYSTEM

Chapter fit in overall framework:

Problem	Solution	Epiphany		
		A *broken* system		
Soaring college debt	Get a career, not just a degree, with minimal debt	Career goals - Pursue your passions		
		Estimate your earning potential		
		Choose a school you can afford		
Career uncertainty	Proactively stay employable	Career uncertainty *will* affect you		
		Adopt a mindset that embraces change		
		Keep investing in yourself		
Lack of financial literacy	Learn **why** we *must* save	You *need* compounding		
	Learn **how** to save	*You* control your mindset		
		Save *first*		
		Live for *today* - "What's your butter?"		
	Learn **what** to do with savings	It's *not* too intimidating		

Have you ever noticed how meetings at work tend to generate more meetings in a self-perpetuating manner akin to a bureaucratic system? This chapter looks at **the system** involved in the college selection decision making process. There are multiple *players* in this system: the federal government (the direct source of almost all student loans), colleges and universities, influencers like high school counselors and consultants, and the student and family. **There is a self-perpetuating nature to this system which drives and supports ever higher costs of attendance.** The engineer in me sees a system that is not producing a desired result; I call that a broken system.

CHAPTER EPIPHANY – A BROKEN SYSTEM

I think the current process to select a college results in **many students and parents making emotional decisions to choose schools they really can't afford. In doing so, they borrow excessive amounts of debt**. I want you to be able to recognize and navigate what is wrong in this system. I also want you to be open to the possibility of avoiding the system entirely – pursuing another path such as a community college, trade school, apprenticeship, or entrepreneurship.

A Broken System – A Self-Perpetuating Cycle

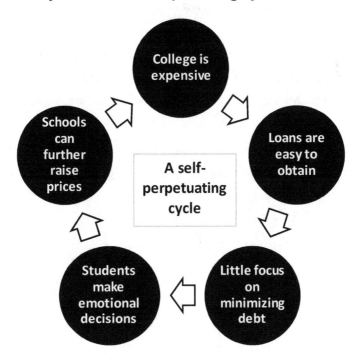

Before we take a closer look at each part of this self-perpetuating cycle, let's review **the outcomes associated with the current environment**[5]:

- Total student loan debt is increasing astronomically and **now exceeds $1.5 trillion!** This does not include second mortgages and hits to retirement savings by parents to fund college.

- **Nearly a third of this college debt is non-performing:** either delinquent or deferred. Such a high percentage of total student loans that are non-performing is a massive percentage in the world of finance, especially compared to the non-performing ratio for corporate debt, even in recessions.

- **Student loan debt is both the fastest growing** and **the second biggest category of consumer debt,** trailing only mortgage debt. Student loan debt now exceeds both auto loans and credit card debt.

- **Lastly, the personal impacts we have mentioned:** Graduates are entering the workforce, or trying to enter the workforce, with excessive debt, and thus in no position to save money. Many parents, also with excessive debt, are being forced to reconsider or abandon their dreams of retirement.

Expanding on the previous diagram - The current environment is a broken system characterized by a self-perpetuating cycle:

College is expensive	The cost to attend college is high, and as it has for decades, is rising multiples of the rate of inflation.
Loans are easy to obtain	**Federal student loans are very easy to obtain.** Federal **loans are issued** *without* **consideration of career objectives, progress towards on-time graduation and employment, or analysis of a student's future earning power** needed to pay off the loans. The federal government, directly through the Department of Education, administers over 90% of all student loans. However, there are limits on how much a student can borrow from the federal government, so for many schools there is still a large funding gap. This gap is often filled when the government issues loans to parents called **Parent PLUS loans;** these **can be taken out up to the full cost of attendance and come with a large upfront fee**.
There is little focus on minimizing debt	**Players in the system often help the student get what they want** (e. g. the campus or name) instead of what they need (e.g. a degree and career with minimal debt).
Students make emotional decisions	Sadly, students and families **all too often simply *fall in love* with a campus** or are swayed by communication with the schools. In the end they make a largely emotional decision to attend a school they truly cannot afford.
Schools have the opportunity to further raise prices	Schools have the opportunity to raise the cost of attendance **knowing those families who have the means will pay while those who do not will obtain loans**. The uncapped nature of the parent loans especially feeds into the ability of schools to raise the cost. Schools are **also in a spending arms race to invest in campus amenities and staff to catch the prospective student's eye**. Schools further raise the price of attendance to obtain a return on this investment… *perpetuating the cycle.*

Cost of Attendance and What You Pay

My introduction highlighted the truly astonishing costs of attendance (COA) families face today.

- Many private schools cost over $50,000 per year with some as high as $80,000 per year. The average private school costs about $30,000 per year.

- State schools average about $10,000 per year with many above $25,000.

- Multiply these annual costs by 4-5 times to estimate your total cost to get an undergraduate degree!

- Always understand the difference in cost between in-state and out-of-state and tuition and room and board. Room and board are surprisingly expensive.

I need to acknowledge that the full COA is rarely what you have to pay. Some families, with the means to pay, and many international students *do* end up paying the *full sticker price*. **The fact that students frequently pay different amounts to attend the same college is part of this frustrating and *devilish* system; it is a very effective price discriminator.**

In this system a college will start with the COA and compute something called the expected family contribution (EFC). The EFC is an opaque and complicated formula that factors in a family's income and some of its assets and how many children are in the family. The purpose of this formula is to determine financial aid eligibility. The gap (COA – EFC) is filled mostly with loans. I believe **the expected family contribution approach does not communicate the concerted effort to minimize loans and debt that I promote**.

Next - Minimizing and avoiding loans may mean some schools are out of reach or that you should consider an alternative path. We address this potentially harsh reality in the next three chapters. I also provide a specific plan for approaching how to pay for college.

CHAPTER TWO

CAREER GOALS - PURSUE YOUR PASSIONS

Chapter fit in overall framework:

Problem	Solution	Epiphany
Soaring college debt	Get a career, not just a degree, with minimal debt	A *broken* system
		Career goals - Pursue your passions
		Estimate your earning potential
		Choose a school you can afford
Career uncertainty	Proactively stay employable	Career uncertainty *will* affect you
		Adopt a mindset that embraces change
		Keep investing in yourself
Lack of financial literacy	Learn **why** we *must* save	You *need* compounding
	Learn **how** to save	*You* control your mindset
		Save *first*
		Live for *today* - "What's your butter?"
	Learn **what** to do with savings	It's *not* too intimidating

I *didn't* consider my passions when I was 18. My dad was an engineer. My brother was away studying to be an engineer. I did well on the math SAT. So, I blindly decided to pursue engineering, too. When I entered the workforce, at least initially, I definitely did not enjoy being an engineer.

If I actually had considered my passions in high school, I may have connected some dots...my love of baseball, my analytical and mathematical skills, and a budding trend in professional baseball to look at old statistics in a new way. I could have been on the ground floor of the revolution in baseball analytics, well before the movie *Money Ball*. I could have reported to work at a major league ballpark. I could have interacted with major league players, for a living. It was/is an ultra-competitive field, but now I'll never know!

You can't change the high price to attend some colleges. You can, however, try to avoid taking on too much debt. In this chapter I begin to outline a personal process to minimize college loans, presented as a three-part plan, that starts with you considering your passions.

Overview of Three-Part Plan to Minimize College Debt

1. **Career choice:** I encourage you to deeply consider what is best for you, what fits you, and what you are passionate about. Approach the college decision with the goal and mindset to pursue a career, not just a degree.

2. **Income potential of your career choice:** Your career choice may not be motivated by money; however, it is important to try to estimate what your earning power could be if you achieve your career goals. The point is that future earning potential drives your ability to pay off debt.

3. **School affordability based on earning power:** I contend that in the end your chances of future success in your career and in life rest more with you than the name of the college you attend. If you do decide you need to go to college, you shouldn't consider schools that are so costly that they require more debt than your future income can reasonably support.

CHAPTER EPIPHANY – PURSUE YOUR PASSIONS

"Choose a job you love, and you'll never have to work a day in your life" is an old saying, but still true today. While it sounds obvious, how many discussions with family, friends, school counselors, or college admissions offices **challenge you to think this way?** I hope that by thinking about your passions you will arrive at clear career goals that you will be motivated to achieve.

Assess Career Goals – Pursue Your Passions

I encourage high school students to strongly consider what they should study in college and all that goes into selecting and preparing for a career. I know that when high school students start the college selection process, they are juggling a lot already. They are busy with homework, standardized test prep, after school activities, friends, and in general the *fragmented and short attention span world* we live in. It is hard to step back and think of the big picture and long-term horizon. But if you spend more time actively considering what to pursue in college, **it can pay dividends. With the cost of college so high today, it really is not best to just go to college and *then* explore your options**.

- **Pursue your passions.** If you want a job you love, you should pursue your passions. I beg you to at least consider your passions. **My definition of passion is *no motivation required.*** If you are passionate, you don't need to be prodded, pushed, and nagged to get something done; you will want to do it and it will get done. To figure out what your passions are, ask yourself:

  - What are your skills, interests, talents, and gifts?

  - What are your values?

  - What **drives** you?

  - Do you need to *shadow* someone in a field of interest to learn more?

- *Do what you love,* **or maximize income?** As you consider your passions, you should also **explicitly consider how important money is to you.** Is your goal to do something you love regardless of income, to maximize income, or somewhere in between? The reality is that you may be unhappy if you force yourself into a high-paying job just for the money. Or you may use your passion in a low-paying field to turn such an opportunity into more income than you ever expected.

- **Are you potentially an entrepreneur?** Ask yourself: are you someone who wants to start your own business and work for yourself?
  **I am not suggesting it is one or the other, become an entrepre-
  neur or go to college; in fact, it typically is not.** A desire to become an entrepreneur though **may impact your college choice or
  selection of classes.** Consider these pros and cons:

Pros	A clear opportunity to pursue your passions, flexibility, being your own boss, and keeping the rewards of your work.
Cons	The fact that many small businesses fail and there is no employer sharing the risks and costs (e.g. healthcare).

- **Is college right for you?** To cover all our bases, we should include
  some other considerations. **College is not for everyone!** Some people may prefer trade schools or working as an apprentice with an
  experienced tradesman. For example, your passion may be electri-
  cal work, plumbing, carpentry, car repair or refurbishment, etc. **Be
  honest with yourself** and make sure you consider all options if these
  are the areas where your passions lie. You might know the television
  personality Mike Rowe, mostly from the Discovery Channel show
  Dirty Jobs; he is very articulate on this topic. You can check out his
  sites https://www.mikeroweworks.org/ and http://mikerowe.com/.

- **Do you *know*, upfront, the degree or level of education you
  need in order to get the job you want?** As you zero in on your
  stated career goals, it is good to know upfront the full educational
  requirements for that job. Is an associate degree or certificate sufficient? Do you need a bachelor's degree, a master's degree, or PhD?
  Perhaps a high school diploma is enough. Considering this level of
  detail exposes some options with financial implications:

  - Knowing upfront that you will very likely need a master's degree
    could impact your undergraduate college selection decision. Fu-
    ture employers may look more at where you earned your mas-
    ter's degree and not your undergraduate degree. Plus, acceptance
    into the master's program is likely more to do with grades at the

undergraduate level and the entrance exam scores than where you attended undergraduate school. **So, if you are fairly certain that you will need a master's degree, why take on crippling amounts of undergraduate debt?**

- Discovering that your career goals require a 2-year degree or certificate and not a 4-year program presents an obvious opportunity to save.

- Some students transfer from one school to another prior to graduation. Many transfers are because the student determined they did not like their first choice or because they changed career goals. However, some have a plan all along to **start out at a less expensive community college** (e.g. for the first two years) **then transfer to another college, which appears on their diploma**. **This strategy produces significant savings. This approach also helps high school students who have marginal grades.** Successfully completing two years at a community college essentially gives such a student a clean slate, becoming a proven college student with good grades to get accepted and to finish at a four-year college.

ACTIVITY - CAREER GOALS CHECKLIST

"Choose a job you love, and you'll never have to work a day in your life."

1. Explore what you *love* to do.
   - What are you passionate about? (passion means no motivation required)
   - What are your skills, interests, talents, gifts, values?
   - What drives and motivates you?
2. Consider how important money is to you. Would you rather:
   - Maximize your income
   - *Do what you love* regardless of income
   - Somewhere in between
3. Are you potentially an entrepreneur?
   - Do you have a desire to start and run your own business?
4. Are you sure college is right for you? Is your true passion typically attained via a different path?
5. How much schooling do you need (e.g. associate degree, certificate, bachelor's degree, master's degree, PhD, etc.)? How should this impact your school choice?

Next - The next chapter continues with my three-part plan to pursue a career and/or the degree you want while minimizing student debt.

CHAPTER THREE

Estimate Your Earning Potential

Chapter fit in overall framework:

Problem	Solution	Epiphany
Soaring college debt	Get a career, not just a degree, with minimal debt	A *broken* system
		Career goals - Pursue your passions
		Estimate your earning potential
		Choose a school you can afford
Career uncertainty	Proactively stay employable	Career uncertainty *will* affect you
		Adopt a mindset that embraces change
		Keep investing in yourself
Lack of financial literacy	Learn **why** we *must* save	You *need* compounding
	Learn **how** to save	*You* control your mindset
		Save *first*
		Live for *today* - "What's your butter?"
	Learn **what** to do with savings	It's *not* too intimidating

Think of your income potential as indicative of *your* ability to take on and service debt. To illustrate, think of iconic brands: Coke, Pepsi, a Disney character, Band Aids, Kleenex, etc. For some real or perceived reason, we are willing to pay more for these brands versus their competitors. The companies that own these brands capitalize on their brand recognition during both good and bad economic times. **The high and stable cash generation allows these companies to take on more debt** (i.e., to borrow more) than their competitors. That debt allows them to invest in new plants, R&D, marketing, and other ways to increase their already strong competitive positions. This illustrates how market share begets market share. Can we apply this logic to our process to minimize college debt? The last chapter recommended that you focus on your career objectives as the first part of a three-part plan to minimize debt. This chapter presents part two of the plan: estimate your future income potential.

> **CHAPTER EPIPHANY – ESTIMATE YOUR INCOME POTENTIAL**
>
> Your future earning power determines your ability to pay off student debt.

Estimate Your Earning Potential

After considering your passions to set your career goals, you need to estimate the earning power associated with those goals. **Your earning power determines your ability to pay off student loans and position yourself to be ready to begin saving at a young age.**

What should you look for in your research?

- **Compensation data:** Look for data on the median salary in the industry, typical *starting* salary, and estimates for salary growth potential.

- **Jobs outlook:** Look for analysis of the future prospects for the sector and industry to gauge career opportunities and income growth potential.

Where Should You Look for Information?

- The Bureau of Labor Statistics:

  - *Occupational Outlook Handbook* at *https://www.bls.gov/ooh/* is an excellent source of information on earning potential and industry outlooks.

  - *Occupational Employment Statistics* database at https://www.bls.gov/oes/current/oes_stru.htm allows you to drill down into specific occupation profiles.

  - *One-Screen data retrieval tool* at https://data.bls.gov/PDQWeb/wm can help you find data that is very geographic location specific.

- High school counselors, public librarians, and service providers (e.g. college consultants) can help you research careers.

Time Out! Reality Check

At this point I acknowledge the obvious, that **this exercise of researching your earning power produces** *at best an estimate.* **Why is it at best an estimate?**

- Precise information may not be available.

- You simply may not yet know the eventual, specific job or application of a broader degree you want to pursue. For example, do you use a biology degree to work in a lab or as a stepping stone to pursue a pre-med track? Or, you pursue a general business degree but don't know if you will end up working for a corporation or non-profit.

- Your career goals may radically change. For example, you may start out studying engineering and switch to economics.

- Salary decisions vary based on applicant-specific personal qualities and also the required cost of living in the area of the country offering the job opportunity.

More importantly, **why is it okay to use an estimate** of earning power?

- **The goal here is a simple *reality check*. I hope to open your eyes to catch potential *extreme outcomes*.** If your self-assessment zeroed in on careers that pay about $30,000 a year, you will have much less ability to pay off debt than most future engineers, computer coders, financial analysts, or many in the medical field, who may start out earning over $60,000 per year. For example, we need many more good teachers, and I encourage students to pursue teaching if that is their passion. While teachers are fortunate to someday receive a pension, lessening their need to save during their working years, the reality is that their starting income level is typically not high, and more importantly, a teacher can attain the same level of salary with less investment (i.e., choosing a less expensive school). A student pursuing a teaching career will have difficulty paying off loans if they attend an expensive private school.

Next - A debt load that can be supported by your earning power **feeds into the schools you can afford and should consider. Choosing a school you can afford** is what we address in **the next chapter.**

CHAPTER FOUR

CHOOSE A SCHOOL YOU CAN AFFORD

Chapter fit in overall framework:

Problem	Solution	Epiphany
Soaring college debt	Get a career, not just a degree, with minimal debt	A *broken* system
		Career goals - Pursue your passions
		Estimate your earning potential
		Choose a school you can afford
Career uncertainty	Proactively stay employable	Career uncertainty *will* affect you
		Adopt a mindset that embraces change
		Keep investing in yourself
Lack of financial literacy	Learn **why** we *must* save	You *need* compounding
	Learn **how** to save	*You* control your mindset
		Save *first*
		Live for *today* - "What's your butter?"
	Learn **what** to do with savings	It's *not* too intimidating

Think again about those iconic brands. Now imagine instead a start-up with no proven technology, commercial product, or revenue/income stream. Or consider a company that produces a commodity like steel or oil. Commodity companies can earn a lot in good times, but they can see earnings evaporate in a recession when demand falls. Compared to the iconic brands, which generate high and *steady* cashflow, the unproven start-up and cyclical commodity producers generate **inconsistent cashflow and can't support much debt** as there will be times when they can't make debt payments.

I am advocating for a personal plan for a student to get the career and degree they need without crippling amounts of student or parent college debt. The plan includes a three-part solution which begins with the student deeply considering their career goals. Next, the student estimates the future earning power of such a career.

So, after deciding on your career goals and estimating your earning power or income potential, do you look more like Coke or more like a commodity producer? That is, **do you expect a fairly high starting salary that can support college debt or a low/uncertain income that cannot pay off much debt? This chapter will help you understand how to determine which schools you can afford.**

CHAPTER EPIPHANY – CHOOSE A SCHOOL YOU CAN AFFORD

The key is to take the emotion out of this important decision. To do that, you need a repeatable process. I provide a specific mathematical rule of thumb to *size* the student's debt load, and based on this, I encourage you **to choose a school you can afford!**

Choose a School You Can Afford

To be successful at choosing a school you can afford, you should begin by only *looking* at schools you can afford. Importantly, decide **this early** so you don't visit other schools that will tempt you to make a purely emotional decision. Don't underestimate the potential to be tempted. It is hard not to fall in love with a beautiful college campus when visiting on a gorgeous autumn day.

My message suggesting that you only look at schools you can afford **sounds harsh and is likely unpopular.** It sounds **limiting.** It may even sound **unfair. I simply care about your future financial situation.**

Remember our goals:

1. I encourage **students to *minimize* college loan debt** so they can build wealth in their 20s and leverage compounding! Remember that there is likely a long list of schools you can choose from to get the degree you need for your chosen career goals. Frankly, your initial list of potential schools may be based on superficial reasons or allegiances that, in the end, may not be worth taking on excessive debt. I also firmly believe that **your future success is more about *you* than the name of the college you attend.** If you are a high-performer, anywhere, you are likely to succeed in your future endeavors.

2. I want **parents to contribute to paying for college from savings specifically set aside *for college*** (i.e., not retirement savings). I also **encourage parents to *avoid* college debt.** Parent college debt, which can explode due to the uncapped nature of Parent PLUS loans, can derail the parent's retirement finances, timing, and dreams.

Paying for College - Funding Sources (My Suggested Rank Order)

There are various ways to pay for college. Most families use a combination of means. Here is a list of funding sources in *my suggested rank order*:

- **Free money:** Your first priority, to reduce the out of pocket cost of attendance, should be to search for and maximize *free money*: **money you do not have to pay back**. This includes **grant money and scholarships**. Start by researching whether your schools of interest offer merit scholarships. **Merit scholarships are a sign a school *wants you* –** that is valuable to know. Also, it can be in your interest to **write an appeal letter** to your school of choice advising them of and **leveraging** offers of merit scholarships from other schools. Don't forget you can keep writing appeal letters for subsequent years as well, as schools want to keep you as opposed to having to search for transfer students to fill seats and beds. Next, you'd be amazed how many scholarships are available if *you* spend the time digging and applying. Many are available from local sources specific to your community. The flip side is that most are *very* small.

- **Work study:** If you find that you are eligible, you can also apply for a work study opportunity which can help you contribute a few thousand dollars.

- **Family savings:** Next comes what the family has saved, **referring to savings earmarked for college, not retirement. College savings often fall *far short,*** leaving a large funding gap for some schools; too few parents share this fact with the student.

- **Loans:** The remaining gap must be filled with loans. Again, my goal is to motivate you to *minimize* student loans and *avoid* parent loans. **My advice is to *size* student loans based on future earning potential, as an indicator of a manageable amount of debt.** The following *Insight* box describes the underlying calculation to *size* the total debt load.

INSIGHT – SIZING THE STUDENT DEBT LOAD

An appropriate college debt load is about 1x (one times) the student's estimated future starting salary: the lower the better.

Remember, **debt load is your accumulated total of debt** (i.e. after all two, four, or more years of school). Don't make individual semester or school year debt decisions in isolation. Even early on, calculate and forecast what your total debt load will likely be when you finish school, hopefully graduating on time.

Please know that a fair amount of math and analysis goes into deriving this seemingly simple rule of thumb. I don't want you to have more **college debt than would be manageable.** I also want you still to be in a position to save money at a young age.

Definitely do not exceed 1x if you are likely to have a lower salary. Federal student loans are easily obtained up to a cumulative maximum amount (four-year total amount) of about $27,000. Thus, for some students who expect to be low-income earners (about $30,000), they really shouldn't take on any more loans! Higher expected income (e.g. greater than $50,000) can support a bit more debt but even at 1.25x (debt at 1.25 times the starting salary), annual debt payments will be approaching 20% of gross income!

My analysis is generic and obviously cannot factor in each individual's personal situation. My model and rule of thumb may suggest a safe level of debt but if the individual does not control personal spending, lives in an especially expensive area or city, does not prioritize paying off debt, or does not maintain their earning power, then the individual may still run into problems paying off their college debt.

CAVEATS:

I really do empathize with how students and families may struggle with my advice. I am not suggesting attending college without any borrowing; I am urging you to *minimize* debt. I acknowledge:

- Some parents do take loans to help their children attend college.

- Some parents want their children to have a *financial stake* in going to college, and they see a loan as that stake. That is a reasonable argument, often motivated by a parental desire for children to learn to manage their finances. My experience, however, is that students don't relate to the financial stake of having a loan because the impact is deferred (i.e., the effort, and perhaps even hardship, associated with repayment is too many years in the future past the time of loan disbursement to pay for school). Therefore, the financial lesson parents think they are teaching fails to hit the mark. I'd prefer that graduates be in a position to save and build wealth rather than be in a hole paying off debt.

- Some students and parents can't put aside a dream school or legacy opportunity.

- There is some level of rationalization that some debt is an investment in a higher paying future job.

Students and parents, please don't lose sight of my primary goal which is to help you recognize and avoid a problem that is literally crippling many of your peers. I want you to at least have a framework and personal process to make a better college selection decision than you might otherwise make. My advice is challenging, but I think it is in your best interest in the long run.

Next - I recap Part I.

CHAPTER FIVE

PART I RECAP

Part I fit in overall framework:

Problem	Solution	Epiphany
Soaring college debt	Get a career, not just a degree, with minimal debt	A *broken* system
		Career goals - Pursue your passions
		Estimate your earning potential
		Choose a school you can afford
Career uncertainty	Proactively stay employable	Career uncertainty *will* affect you
		Adopt a mindset that embraces change
		Keep investing in yourself
Lack of financial literacy	Learn **why** we *must* save	You *need* compounding
	Learn **how** to save	*You* control your mindset
		Save *first*
		Live for *today* - "What's your butter?"
	Learn **what** to do with savings	It's *not* too intimidating

Part I identified and described the problems of **a *broken system* characterized by a self-perpetuating cycle that results in and supports ever higher costs of college and the exploding amount of student debt to fund attendance.** The self-perpetuating cycle looks like:

- **College is expensive** with costs rising multiples of the rate of inflation.

- **Loans are easy to obtain.** Federal loans are issued with no consideration of student career goals, progress towards achieving goals, and future income potential for paying back the loans. Loans to parents are literally uncapped up to the full cost of attendance.

- **The focus is not on minimizing debt or the negative implications of debt**. Players in the system help the student get what they want over what they need.

- **Students and families often make emotional decisions**. In the end, students often *fall in love* with a campus or amenities.

- **Schools have the opportunity to further raise prices**. Colleges can keep **raising tuition knowing students will either get loans or that some can pay** at or near full price. Schools are also over-investing in facilities and administrators to catch the eye of the prospective student. A desire to recoup this investment also contributes to rising costs of attendance.

The **results of this broken system are rapidly rising costs to attend college and a student debt bubble as students and families make poor financial decisions when they select schools they really can't afford.** Both students and parents suffer from too much college debt. Student debt means graduates start out in a financial hole and are not in a position to save when they are young. College debt held by parents, easy to occur with the uncapped nature of Parent PLUS loans, can derail retirement plans and endanger financial security.

To provide a personal process to combat the problems, **I proposed a three-part plan:** a roadmap for you to use to set yourself up for success:

1. **Carefully consider your career choice**: I urge students to pursue, or at least consider, their true passions in selecting a future career.

2. **Estimate your future earning power; the premise being that it is your future earning power that is needed to pay off the debt**: An estimate is enough of a reality check to avoid a debt load you *can't possibly* pay back.

3. *Size* **your student debt** based on your estimated future earning power and **only consider schools you can afford: My modeling suggests an appropriate debt load is about 1x the graduate's estimated starting salary. The lower the better.** Definitely do not exceed 1x if you are likely to have a low salary (e.g. $30,000 per year).

My empowering, though *unpopular,* conclusion is to choose a school you can afford. This approach is only possible if you decide early in the college selection process to only *visit* schools you can afford. I encourage open communication between parents and student; talk openly about what the family has saved for college and what the financial implications would be to take on too much debt. **The more you stick to a process, the easier it will be to remove the emotion from this major financial decision.** College is expensive. We can't change that fact. **In the end, it is the student and family's responsibility to make a sound financial decision and select a school they can afford.**

That concludes Part I on minimizing student debt and positioning you to save and build wealth from a young age.

PART II

You Can't Save if You Can't Get and Hold a Good Job

"Every generation gets a chance to change the world."

U2

Part II fit in overall framework:

Problem	Solution	Epiphany
Soaring college debt	Get a career, not just a degree, with minimal debt	A *broken* system
		Career goals - Pursue your passions
		Estimate your earning potential
		Choose a school you can afford
Career uncertainty	Proactively stay employable	Career uncertainty *will* affect you
		Adopt a mindset that embraces change
		Keep investing in yourself
Lack of financial literacy	Learn **why** we *must* save	You *need* compounding
	Learn **how** to save	*You* control your mindset
		Save *first*
		Live for *today* - "What's your butter?"
	Learn **what** to do with savings	It's *not* too intimidating

At 8:30am on the first Friday of every month, the Bureau of Labor Statistics releases the monthly employment report. There is a lot of information in the jobs report. The media tends to focus on the headline unemployment number (i.e., the percent of the labor force currently out of work). Investors, like I used to be, dive into the nuanced data within the report to see which sectors and industries in the broader economy are creating jobs. I bring this up because people often think in purely

black and white terms of being employed or unemployed. The reality is that the unemployment rate is usually quite low at 4-5%. What I think is more relevant to our discussion is being *underemployed*: doing a job that does not make full use of your skills and abilities. How many new graduates do you know who are underemployed: working at a coffee shop, at a restaurant, in a mall, doing landscaping, etc.? **This book is about saving money and building wealth. Unfortunately, you can't save if you can't get and hold a good job.** Part II addresses the problem of career uncertainty occurring in our changing world and offers solutions to **proactively stay employable and to *grow* your income**.

This book provides guidance on how to save money. Techniques on saving often emphasize controlling spending. *Earning more,* **while still controlling spending, can help you save more too. Unfortunately, people today generally have an unclear view of their earnings trajectory because there is great uncertainty about getting, and then holding on to, a job in the first place!**

The message in this section resonates especially well with college students or young adults entering the workforce, who are just beginning to shape a career or an approach to a career. High school students, who are considering career objectives and searching for a college, will also see value in the insight that a degree is not the be all and end all and that long-term employability is about many other factors outside of and beyond school choice and what you learn in school.

I've said, generally, that a sound, repeatable process is a road map for success. I am trying to teach a personal process to be financially literate and, in this section, to stay employable and improve your earning power. **Yet, the process, or nature of holding down a job, and your required approach to a job, are changing in today's world. *When the environment changes, the process needs to evolve*.** Thus, you need to be aware of these changes and ahead of this problem to compete and stay employed.

Let's look at it another way. How about a sports analogy? **The great Wayne Gretzky said, "Don't skate to where the puck *is*, skate to where the puck *is going to be*."** A similar approach with respect to your skills and career moves is what you need in a changing world.

I can personally relate to career uncertainty and the need to proactively stay employable. I have worked in industries that experienced disruptive change. I have had my specific job function disappear overnight. I have had to proactively reinvent myself to keep my job. I am also a parent of two young adults who have graduated from college and now face this changing world. Many of their peers are underemployed, not using the expensive degree for which they paid (or borrowed). Many of my peers feel stressed and trapped in jobs that are no longer secure.

To ensure that you thrive in today's environment, this section will enable you to:

1. **Identify the problems driving career uncertainty.** This is critical because you need to understand that the rules of the game are changing.

2. **Have a personal process to stay employable.** Your solution will incorporate **adopting a mindset that embraces change and an action plan to keep investing in yourself.**

This will be the flow of the section: I will present the problem first and then highlight the solution. This section should not only raise awareness but hopefully a sense of urgency as well, since **adapting to a changing world and a changing work environment is *your* responsibility.** Career uncertainty *will* affect you. I want you to have a personal process, a mindset, a plan, and a set of actions to respond, adapt, and succeed!

CHAPTER SIX

DEFINE THE PROBLEM – CAREER UNCERTAINTY

Chapter fit in overall framework:

Problem	Solution	Epiphany
Soaring college debt	Get a career, not just a degree, with minimal debt	A *broken* system
		Career goals - Pursue your passions
		Estimate your earning potential
		Choose a school you can afford
Career uncertainty	Proactively stay employable	Career uncertainty *will* affect you
		Adopt a mindset that embraces change
		Keep investing in yourself
Lack of financial literacy	Learn **why** we *must* save	You *need* compounding
	Learn **how** to save	*You* control your mindset
		Save *first*
		Live for *today* - "What's your butter?"
	Learn **what** to do with savings	It's *not* too intimidating

Career uncertainty has very negative financial and quality of life implications. This chapter will walk you through the causes and effects of career uncertainty. Being able to identify a problem affecting you is the first step in your efforts to adapt and cope with the problem.

CHAPTER EPIPHANY – CAREER UNCERTAINTY WILL AFFECT YOU

This chapter prepares you for an inevitability, not merely a possibility.

Drivers of the Problem - Why is There Career Uncertainty?

- **Technological change, automation, artificial intelligence, innovative disruption:** An important driver of career uncertainty in today's world is technological change. Think about jobs that are disappearing, or at least changing, due to technological advances, automation, artificial intelligence, or machine learning. Maybe we all like E-ZPass and don't lose sleep over the lost toll booth attendant jobs. But what's next? What if artificial intelligence displaces all or most pharmacists, doctors, attorneys, or engineers? These are some of our economy's highest paying jobs. Maybe a computer really can perform these jobs better than a human because it remembers *all* the drug interactions, *all* the symptoms, *all* the legal precedence, and *all* the formulas. The reality is that specific jobs and whole industries are constantly facing disruption due to some technological innovation.

- **Globalization and increased job competition:** Another driver of career uncertainty is the globalization of trade and business. This has opened up and connected markets more than ever before. The net result is an increase in job competition. I used to work for someone who'd quite frequently say, "Tyburski, three billion people want your job."

- **Wage stagnation:** Wage stagnation contributes to career uncertainty. A lack of rising wages is partly a result of what I have mentioned so far, technology and job competition reducing labor's power to make demands. People used to count on a steady march of wage increases for a given job description.

- **Overall skills gap:** Another driver of uncertainty is a skills gap as many people in the workforce don't have the skills required in a more technology-driven and service-based economy. The problem goes beyond just the inability of many to adjust and compete for the new jobs. The problem extends to the fact that many lower pay-ing jobs, which used to act as a safety net, are vanishing.

- **Demographics:** Demographics also have an impact on career un-certainty. Millennials are a very large demographic cohort, in fact on par with the baby boomer generation, but opportunities are opening up slowly for them. This is because boomers are not retir-ing as soon as anticipated because the 2008 global financial crisis hit their income and retirement nest eggs.

Summarizing the Effects of Career Uncertainty

- To the **individual and family:** Impacts include anxiety, stagnation, potential loss of income, and the risk of being left behind.
- To **society and the economy:** At an aggregate level the underlying uncertainty manifests in the broad economy being less dynamic, flexible and competitive, and having a lower growth potential.

ACTIVITY – AWARENESS OF CAREER UNCERTAINTY

Can you think of:

- Jobs that *have been eliminated* by technological change or global competition?

- Jobs *at risk* of disappearing or radically changing *going forward*?

- Jobs that may be relatively *well positioned or shielded* from these threats?

Jobs eliminated by technology and global competition: There are many examples. I already mentioned the tollbooth attendant. ATMs reduce the need for as many bank tellers. Robots are replacing jobs in factories and warehouses. Developing countries are manufacturing items that used to be made domestically; this also impacts supply chains and distribution models. Online shopping is taking sales from local shops. Disruptive technology is all around us, changing entire industries. The music industry changed its mode of delivery, and now television is doing the same. When I was a kid, everyone watched *Seinfeld* at 8pm on Thursdays, with many commercials per episode. Now, you watch what you want, when you want, streamed to any device. Trust me, that is a radical disruption. Other examples of radical disruption in everyday life include the impacts of the search engine and free exchange of information to sell new and used items, buy event tickets, and find a date, job, apartment, place for a vacation, a meal review, or a ride around the city. What may seem like ordinary features of today's world are actually radical changes compared to only a few years ago.

Jobs at risk going forward: The next wave of technology could move from simply changing factory floor jobs to posing a real threat to what I call *thought workers*; engineers, doctors, attorneys, etc. In our lifetimes we will see industry innovation and disruption such as self-driving cars and trucks, new energy sources, robotic personal assistants, new ways to wage war, new ways to feed ourselves, and healthcare breakthroughs. These changes will displace and redefine many jobs.

Jobs that may be relatively better positioned: Of course, the jobs associated with the disruptive change are safer than those being displaced. Coders and developers are likely to remain in high demand. There may even be a resurgence of some old skills, made valuable again, precisely because the machines will never be able to fully match humans; e.g. in the areas of expressing empathy and in really communicating and connecting with people. If this proves true, jobs in healthcare and senior care could thrive. Also, creative jobs like writing and conceiving of new entertainment content may be in high demand to fill the new modes of media content distribution.

Next - Now that you are aware of what we are facing, I'll outline how to confront career uncertainty.

CHAPTER SEVEN

ADOPT A MINDSET THAT EMBRACES CHANGE

Chapter fit in overall framework:

Problem	Solution	Epiphany
Soaring college debt	Get a career, not just a degree, with minimal debt	A *broken* system
		Career goals - Pursue your passions
		Estimate your earning potential
		Choose a school you can afford
Career uncertainty	Proactively stay employable	Career uncertainty *will* affect you
		Adopt a mindset that embraces change
		Keep investing in yourself
Lack of financial literacy	Learn **why** we *must* save	You *need* compounding
	Learn **how** to save	*You* control your mindset
		Save *first*
		Live for *today* - "What's your butter?"
	Learn **what** to do with savings	It's *not* too intimidating

This chapter begins a discussion about solutions to career uncertainty. We can't alter the pace of change or the impact of these forces. We can, however, arm ourselves with a personal plan to adapt and survive in this environment.

My recommended solution to career uncertainty is to *proactively* stay employable. More specifically, my solution, and what I address in this and the next chapter, is **a combination of:**

1. **Adopting a <u>mindset</u> that embraces change**, and

2. **Taking <u>specific actions</u> to keep investing in yourself.**

> **CHAPTER EPIPHANY – "NOBODY OWES YOU A CAREER."**
>
> Adopting a mindset that embraces change begins with a realization and revelation that it is **your** responsibility to adapt and survive in a changing world.

"Nobody owes you a career" [6]

I want to share with you how I came to develop this perspective and framework. It's a personal story of how *I* began to proactively stay employable. The catalyst for me was a single line from a book. Andy Grove, founder of Intel, in his book, *Only the Paranoid Survive*, wrote, "Nobody owes you a career."

I kid you not, when I read this book in the mid-1990s, it literally changed my life and sent me in a new direction. I consider that an epiphany moment! Afterwards, I went to night school to get an MBA, and I eventually switched careers. I switched from engineering to finance, working as an investment analyst.

Only the Paranoid Survive **is all about adapting and surviving.** The background story for the book is:

- In 1994, customers discovered a flaw in an Intel computer processing chip. Imagine that, a chip that made a mathematical error.

- Intel's response angered customers.

- The subsequent corporate upheaval and crisis drove Intel's CEO to later write the book.

- **The book has broader messages about the relationship between companies and employees and how to be an employee in today's world.**

The **key message** I took away from reading this book is, **in a changing world** (due to technology, globalization, etc.) **companies can't guarantee employment because they can't guarantee their own survival. So, staying employed is *your* responsibility.**

Let's read from the page that inspired me. These quotes come from a speech Andy Grove delivered to Intel employees. He didn't mince his words!

QUOTES...

"Who knows what your job will look like after cataclysmic change sweeps through your industry and engulfs the company you work for? Who knows if your job will even exist and, frankly, who will care besides you?"

"The sad news is, nobody owes you a career. Your career is literally your business. You own it as a sole proprietor. You have one employee: yourself. You are in competition with millions of similar businesses: millions of other employees all over the world. You need to accept ownership of your career, your skills and the timing of your moves. It is your responsibility to protect this personal business of yours from harm and to position it to benefit from the changes in the environment. Nobody else can do that for you."

Words like that terrified people back in the 1990s, a time when many workers were accustomed to lifetime employment. At that time, reality was starting to sink in. Corporate downsizing was spitting out 10,000 people at a time on to the streets. The term downsizing was possibly coined in my hometown of Rochester, NY, by film manufacturer Kodak. Kodak proved to be a case study on an iconic, dominant brand facing technological obsolescence associated with digital cameras.

Today, the uncertainty of the employment environment is less about waves of downsizing (i.e., staying employed) and more about getting and keeping a job in a changing world (i.e., staying employable).

Extracting the key points from Andy Grove's quotes:

- Own your career like it's a sole proprietorship.
- **Your *business* is you**...I think that is a cool perspective. Even if you work for a large Fortune 500 company, you can have an entrepreneur's mindset that embraces change.
- **Position and protect your *business*** to benefit in a changing world.
- **Keep yourself marketable and flexible.**
- **Control the timing of your job or career moves.**

Next - With a mindset that embraces change, we are ready to **talk about specific actions to proactively stay employable.**

CHAPTER EIGHT

KEEP INVESTING IN YOURSELF

Chapter fit in overall framework:

Problem	Solution	Epiphany
Soaring college debt	Get a career, not just a degree, with minimal debt	A *broken* system
		Career goals - Pursue your passions
		Estimate your earning potential
		Choose a school you can afford
Career uncertainty	Proactively stay employable	Career uncertainty *will* affect you
		Adopt a mindset that embraces change
		Keep investing in yourself
Lack of financial literacy	Learn **why** we *must* save	You *need* compounding
	Learn **how** to save	*You* control your mindset
		Save *first*
		Live for *today* - "What's your butter?"
	Learn **what** to do with savings	It's *not* too intimidating

Here, we will build on the marching orders given to us by Andy Grove. I will provide a personal game plan for you to proactively stay employable. This chapter will use a common format, pairing the mindset you must adopt with the actions required to make it happen.

CHAPTER EPIPHANY – KEEP INVESTING IN YOURSELF

Adopting a mindset that embraces change is only a first step to coping with the changing world. To truly adapt and survive we need to proactively take steps to stay employable and also to improve our earning power. Many of the steps we must take are in the areas of **soft skills** and learning on the job and in life. Keep investing in yourself outside of and beyond school.

Expect to Change Jobs or Even Careers

A mindset that embraces change begins by adopting a realistic perspective that fits this changing world we live in. Specifically, *expect* to change jobs or even careers; don't be shocked, surprised, or threatened when you face the need for change.

Actions to support this mindset:

- **Be proactive** and not caught off guard and reactive.
- **View your career as a building portfolio**. Commit to your current job while you constantly build skills.
- **Be fluid**. Be open and willing to move laterally within a company or receptive to relocation.

Expect to Have to be Your Own Advocate

Don't let yourself fall through the cracks. Realize that in a fast-paced, results-driven, technology-driven world, you will have to be your own agent, advocating for yourself and promoting your accomplishments and qualifications.

Actions to support this mindset:

- **Be your own brand manager**. Think of it as developing your own personal brand and having to act as your own brand ambassador. Your brand is more than the technical stuff on your resume. Your brand includes your skills, your values, and what motivates you. Craft, and learn to articulate, your message.
- **What are you passionate about?** I define passion as *no motivation required*. What is it that you literally love to do? Remember the old adage, "If you love what you do, you never work a day in your life." Look inward and challenge yourself. You will be rewarded in the long run doing what you love.

- **Know your *generic skill set*.** For example, you may be an accountant, but you may have a unique ability to organize and run a complicated project. You may be an engineer, but you may have a unique ability to explain and articulate complex concepts in a straightforward way. What I call generic skills represent your skills at your core, skills you'd display no matter where you worked.

- **Soft skills** are increasingly important to get and hold a job as well as to advance. Soft skills include:

  - Your ability to communicate effectively in written and verbal form.

  - Your ability to truly listen.

  - Your ability to connect the dots and solve problems.

  - Your ability to influence others, to negotiate, to manage.

  - Finally, underlying this whole section, your ability to adapt to change is critical.

I once had a manager and mentor who often said that your intelligence quotient or raw intelligence (IQ) is obviously important, but your emotional quotient (EQ) helps you advance. EQ includes soft skills such as an individual's ability to identify and evaluate a situation and control and express one's emotions. EQ is thus a lot about communication skills, decision making ability, and leadership.

Understand Your Degree is Not the Be All and End All

Another important realization is the mindset that your degree is not the be all and end all that defines your skill set or capabilities. Don't pigeonhole yourself to what is printed on the diploma. It's true, you have innate skills, that generic skill set I just spoke about, but **you also need a lifelong focus on learning and desire and commitment to develop your skills. Constantly demonstrate to people around you - colleagues, managers, and customers - your intellectual curiosity.**

Actions to support this mindset:

- **Be sure to learn on the job and in life.** I emphatically encourage you to learn outside of school. The next two bullets will expand on this and in the process, borderline contradict each other. First, I emphasize the value in, and effort required in, developing a true expertise. Then, I emphasize the value in keeping your options open. There is no one right answer. Life is a balancing act. You may have to do a bit of both or at least be aware of both paths.

- **Becoming an expert: understand Malcolm Gladwell's 10,000 hours rule**[7]. This *rule* defines how many hours in a particular skill you need to become a true expert. Obtaining a job is not the end but rather the beginning of the race. You will need to keep pace with the changes in your industry by identifying and tracking industry sources and trends - not just for opportunities but for threats. Attend conferences. Follow webinars, podcasts, and social media of industry leaders. Spot trends in technology and growth opportunities that point you in the areas you must develop skills.

- **Keep your options open; continuously develop skills in line with your interests and also push the limits of your comfort zone and skill set.**

  - My son has always been one for having laser focused goals. He studied internationally, worked in Africa at a young age, and continues to develop his credentials for a career requiring a global perspective and skills. To hone his skills in line with these interests, he keeps his French fresh by reading French news sites, daily! He has also made some big decisions specifically aimed at ensuring a broad exposure to what he learns and the opportunities he sees.

  - My daughter who, I say proudly, graduated college in less than four years, has degrees in writing and film studies and a certificate in digital media but is particularly intrigued by website design, one part of one of her degrees. She now goes out of her way to practice website design on her own time. She is in that balancing act deciding between narrow and broad and keeping her options open while she builds a broader skill set.

- As you work to proactively develop your skills, you should occasionally, consciously, step outside your comfort zone as well. This might be as simple as volunteering for a new project at work which offers a chance to challenge yourself in new ways and to stand out if you succeed. You may also explicitly seek out and ask for a mentor.

INSIGHT – MY STORY: TO PROACTIVELY STAY EMPLOYED

Here is my personal story. **I present it more as an example of applying what we just covered, rather than thinking my story is worthy of being told**. This is mostly a story of just how frequently I realized that I wasn't the smartest person in the room, yet I had the mindset and drive to evolve. My son uses the March madness phrase "survive and move on": that has always been my goal.

- I started as a design-oriented engineer, quickly realizing this was not the best application of my engineering degree.

- I proactively switched to become a *field* engineer, working in power plants, paper mills, steel mills, and chemical plants. I found it exciting being out in the plants and I excelled at tweaking efficiency out of existing processes.

- When investing and financial markets became a serious hobby of mine, I decided to formalize this effort by earning an MBA in finance at night school.

- Then, I switched careers, not just jobs; I became an industry analyst for a money manager. I was an industry expert covering the industries I used to spend time in as an engineer. I liked working in plants, now I *covered* them. It was a good fit.

- After switching to finance, I earned the CFA designation, which required a self-paced study regimen and a series of difficult pass-fail exams.

- Next, I took on a new opportunity to be a portfolio manager, but that made me a generalist, which I didn't enjoy and didn't excel at. I needed to deliver new value, to somewhat reinvent myself to stay employed. I started spending time acting as a research department liaison, supporting the sales force because I could describe our complex investment strategies to clients and prospects. That proved to be a unique skill.

- Then, I applied that ability to summarize our strategies to create an internal curriculum and school to teach new analysts and interns. The firm's founder loved this display of initiative and the training school was a big success.

- Now with my financial literacy educational service, I think I leverage my whole career - the engineer in me created the framework, the analyst identified the problems to be solved, and the mentor/teacher gets to teach. Frankly, some of this is out of my comfort zone, but I push ahead.

I was an engineer and analyst with an MBA and CFA – rather analytical, math and results-driven attributes. But in the end, what *kept me alive* and evolving were softer skills.

I also encourage you to draw on other life experiences. I am president of a non-profit working with aspiring entrepreneurs in Africa. This 15-year effort has taught me how to work with and draw from people with different skill sets and styles. Exposure to and experience with differing views and approaches proved valuable to me. I gained these insights specifically from experiences outside work as engineering departments and investment firms tend to hire whole groups of people who are very similar. My faith-based non-profit group, and working with a different culture over 7,000 miles away, opened my eyes and broadened my skills working with people towards a mutual goal. The project has also been very rewarding. We have created over 10,000 new jobs and 2,000 new businesses. The locals own and implement the process making it truly sustainable as they expand to communities in three African countries now.

Most important to me has been my family. I've enjoyed being a parent and have been overwhelmed by how much I have learned *from* my kids. They are passionate people and that passion rubs off. I made career decisions with my family in mind. My priority was to eat dinner with my kids and to coach little league and attend events. That didn't fit the culture where I worked, where people stayed late into the evening. I simply did my thing, compensating for going home earlier than others by going into work earlier than most.

You can control your path more than you think! You can build your skills and highlight your generic and soft skills. **Trust me, it doesn't all come down to the degree you obtained, where you went to school, and what is on your resume.**

Next - I will recap Part II.

CHAPTER NINE

PART II RECAP

Part II fit in overall framework:

Problem	Solution	Epiphany
Soaring college debt	Get a career, not just a degree, with minimal debt	A *broken* system
		Career goals - Pursue your passions
		Estimate your earning potential
		Choose a school you can afford
Career uncertainty	Proactively stay employable	Career uncertainty *will* affect you
		Adopt a mindset that embraces change
		Keep investing in yourself
Lack of financial literacy	Learn **why** we *must* save	You *need* compounding
	Learn **how** to save	*You* control your mindset
		Save *first*
		Live for *today* - "What's your butter?"
	Learn **what** to do with savings	It's *not* too intimidating

Part II addressed career uncertainty created by our changing world. I outlined specific drivers of career uncertainty, including technological change, globalization, wage stagnation, skills gaps, and demographics. Career uncertainty has broad implications and spill-over effects on people's ability to save, and even their health. My goal is to arm you with a personal process to combat these forces.

My solution to the problem of career uncertainty **is for you to proactively stay employable, by:**

1. **Adopting a mindset that embraces change.**

2. **Taking specific actions to keep investing in yourself.**

The first step is to adopt a realistic perspective and a mindset that embraces change. Don't be surprised or intimidated by change. *Expect* and welcome change. *Expect* to change jobs or even careers. **The epiphany moment is when you realize you must adopt an attitude, approach, and mindset that "nobody owes you a career," and that it is *your* responsibility, and nobody else's, to ensure you stay employable.** Owning up to this responsibility can mean viewing your career like it is a sole proprietorship and constantly positioning your *business* (you) to benefit in a changing world. Adopting such a perspective changed the course of my career and life. I hope it is a powerful insight and call to action for you too.

In addition to adopting a mindset that welcomes and embraces change, I urge you to **keep investing in yourself** to stay employable. Specific actions you can take include:

- Be proactive, not reactive.
- View your career as an evolving portfolio.
- Be flexible within an organization and open to relocating.
- Be your own brand manager. Understand your brand, and be able to articulate what motivates you, your skills, and what you are passionate about.
- Understand your *generic skill set* and *soft skills* that go beyond what is reflected in the technical skills on your resume.
- Understand that your degree is not the be all and end all and accept that you will constantly have to learn on the job and in life. Show others you have a focus on learning.
- Develop skills in line with your interests.

Hopefully, at this point in the book, you see and agree that **it is *your* responsibility to take these actions. No one can do it for you.** As you see from my own story, **a career path is truly a path, often winding**

and taking big turns. The process really is like climbing a mountain because it takes a lot of effort. It may even force you out of your comfort zone. The constant self-assessments and exercises to articulate your strengths and to improve your skills will be rewarding and open more doors for you. This part of the book was not meant to intimidate or depress. Rather, Part II is meant to inspire you into a level of awareness and action that improves your outlook, perhaps increases your earning power, and hopefully enhances the quality of your life by increasing the chances that you can save money and achieve your financial goals.

PART III

MAKING DAILY DECISIONS TO SAVE AND BUILD WEALTH

"In the end, we are our choices. Build yourself a great story."

Jeff Bezos, founder Amazon

Part III fit in overall framework:

Problem	Solution	Epiphany
Soaring college debt	Get a career, not just a degree, with minimal debt	A *broken* system
		Career goals - Pursue your passions
		Estimate your earning potential
		Choose a school you can afford
Career uncertainty	Proactively stay employable	Career uncertainty *will* affect you
		Adopt a mindset that embraces change
		Keep investing in yourself
Lack of financial literacy	Learn **why** we *must* save	You *need* compounding
	Learn **how** to save	*You* control your mindset
		Save *first*
		Live for *today* - "What's your butter?"
	Learn **what** to do with savings	It's *not* too intimidating

This book is about saving money and building wealth. My focus so far has been on ensuring you are *in a position* to save and build wealth. Part I went deep into helping you avoid crippling student debt. Part II went deep into helping you get and hold a good job and to continuously develop your skills to justify earning more. Avoiding debt and ensuring you remain employable with growing earning power are critical *preconditions* for saving and building wealth. **Now it is time for**

saving and building wealth to be our focus. By the end of this section you will be financially literate: you will know why we must save, how to save, and what to do with your savings.

This section is for anyone who wants a *personal process* to take more control of their lives by saving money and achieving financial goals. When I mention a personal process, I mean it. I believe processes help. I am a process guy having been an engineer and professional investor for over 32 years. A sound, repeatable process is a blueprint for success whether we are talking about building a house or making daily decisions and choices to save and build wealth.

CHAPTER TEN

WHY WE *MUST* SAVE
(YOU *NEED* COMPOUNDING)

Chapter fit in overall framework:

Problem	Solution	Epiphany
Soaring college debt	Get a career, not just a degree, with minimal debt	A *broken* system
		Career goals - Pursue your passions
		Estimate your earning potential
		Choose a school you can afford
Career uncertainty	Proactively stay employable	Career uncertainty *will* affect you
		Adopt a mindset that embraces change
		Keep investing in yourself
Lack of financial literacy	Learn **why** we *must* save	You *need* compounding
	Learn **how** to save	*You* control your mindset
		Save *first*
		Live for *today* - "What's your butter?"
	Learn **what** to do with savings	It's *not* too intimidating

Will you be ready for the future? It's a complex question because you can come at it from multiple perspectives: intellectually, physically, emotionally, spiritually, etc. My perspective, of course, is financially. **Will you be ready, financially, for the future?** If you think of the typical events and milestones that lie ahead in life, are you going to be ready for those expenses? **The first thought that comes to my head is that the only way to be ready is to think ahead and plan**.

A tragedy happened while I was writing this chapter: Notre Dame Cathedral in Paris burned. I can't stop thinking about it. I share everyone's sadness. I feel bad for Paris, France, the Catholic Church, and humanity for the loss of a notable monument (in its original form). My son studied a semester in Paris. We, like millions of tourists a year, walked through it. It was incredible, of course, as you'd expect for something that took almost 200 years to build. My sadness, however, quickly morphed into genuine frustration. The fire, or the fact that the fire got so out of control, seems totally preventable to me. Maybe I am just being my normal somewhat harsh and outspoken self, the black and white engineer, etc. I can't help but ask, where was the proactive planning to prevent this catastrophe?

Sure, hindsight is 20/20, but it seems to take only about a minute of hindsight and Monday morning quarterbacking to ask some simple yet powerful questions: Why was there such a slow response, with reports many fire trucks took two hours to arrive? Why did they struggle to pump water out of the adjacent river? Why was there no fire suppression system in the wooden roof/attic structure (literally nicknamed *the forest* because of the 850-year-old timber that once occupied over 50 acres)? It just seems to me that for such an irreplaceable structure, which housed even more irreplaceable relics, there would be multiple layers of preventative planning to ensure such a fire could *never* happen. How about fire stations located on the island right next to the church? How about fire brigades rigorously trained to combat a fire in such a unique structure? How about custom designed equipment to aid in firefighting in the high reaches of a gothic church? How about pre-staged pumping equipment by the river or water tanks to ensure an immediate initial response when a fire is still small? How about extra on-site monitoring during a renovation and construction activity? As you can see, I am a bit worked up. Perhaps I am projecting, and I see Notre Dame as representative of a broader problem with governments, countries, businesses, organizations, families, and individuals...we don't plan and prepare, we just react.

Contrast Notre Dame with US Airways flight 1549. Does that ring a bell? Flight 1549 is known as the "miracle on the Hudson". On January 15, 2009, a passenger jet carrying 155 people left LaGuardia

Airport and three minutes into flight, while still climbing, it struck a flock of geese and consequently lost all engine power. Pilot Chesley "Sully" Sullenberger glided the plane to a ditching in the Hudson River off Midtown Manhattan. Was this outcome, which saved all lives on the plane and countless on the heavily populated ground, pure luck? I don't think so. The pilot was a well-trained and experienced former fighter pilot. While the co-pilot rifled through a checklist to try to restart the engines, pilot Sully made the near instantaneous decision that with no power he couldn't make it back to any airport. They ditched in the water and the well-trained flight crew evacuated passengers. The A320 plane was well-designed to float and life rafts operated as intended. Did anyone know beforehand the specific terrifying emergency they would be faced with? Of course not. But through proper planning, design, training, and experience, those involved were prepared for a range of scenarios. People on the ground and in the water mobilized, contributing to the miracle. In the end, a lot had to go right, and it did, for no lives to have been lost. Proper planning clearly played a major role in the happy ending.

Let's circle back to financial literacy. How do we prepare for the future so we can take care of ourselves and our children, give something back to others, and not be dependent on others when we are old? The answer is we save money today!

We *must* save because:

1. We have many **future financial needs** over multiple time horizons.

2. It is **increasingly our responsibility** to provide for our family's future.

3. And perhaps the most important reason we must save is **money can grow**. Thus, the earlier in life you begin to save, the more time your money has to work for you, compounding and growing to meet your future needs.

CHAPTER EPIPHANY – YOU NEED COMPOUNDING

The fact that money can grow is not to be viewed merely as a bonus or a luxury. What you will find, and what many people don't realize, is that **you need your money to grow**. You need the power of compounding because it is unlikely you can set aside enough savings for all future financial needs. To fully benefit from compounding, you should start saving when you are young! Also, inflation erodes future purchasing power and requires some growth in your assets just to maintain your current purchasing power, let alone grow it.

Why Save? For Future Financial Needs

Here, I highlight some important categories of savings everyone should consider. There are so many future needs. It is a bit intimidating to list them all.

- You should have an **emergency fund**, in case, for instance, you lose your job. You should set aside enough money to cover several months of expenses. Remember, in a true emergency you will focus on meeting basic needs and not going to the movies or a gym membership. Focusing on meeting basic needs makes the emergency fund saving goal smaller and achievable.

- You should always be planning for **infrequent bills,** those annual or semi-annual bills, like insurance and property/school taxes. You have to be ready for them, with money already set aside, when these periodic bills come due.

- There may be **some debt you want to prioritize and pay back** *early*, like some student loans or credit card debt with higher interest rates. Frankly, I hope you never have credit card debt, *ever!*

- Of course, you must plan to fund **life's many major events** over the **short, medium, and long-term.** Some of these are exciting bucket list items: a vacation, a wedding, a new car, or your first house. Others, as we already discussed, are daunting long-term responsibilities like saving for your kids to go to college and your retirement.

When we talk later about setting saving goals, it is good to remember this framework. **It is valuable to understand that your saving goals span multiple time horizons.** The gratification, and feeling of accomplishment, of achieving near-term goals can propel you on to eventually meet the long-term goals too.

Future lessons will discuss *how to save*, but with a long list of future needs, **how do you allocate your savings? One strategy is** to think of and employ **a *cascading buckets approach*.** Picture a series of buckets on the steps of a ladder. The top bucket can represent saving for an emergency fund. When that bucket is full, additional savings *overflow* into the next, lower bucket(s). Buckets don't always have to represent the full amount required for a particular savings goal. Some buckets can represent an annual goal or allocation towards long-term goals like college and retirement. Excess savings after the annual allocation to long-term goals can then *spill over* to lower priority, but potentially very rewarding, savings buckets for short-term goals such as a vacation or new car.

Why Save? It is Increasingly Our Responsibility

The second reason why we must save is because it is increasingly our responsibility to do so. That is, it is increasingly our responsibility to fund our future financial needs.

Why is this increasingly the case these days?

- For one, **we are living longer.** A longer life expectancy raises the anxious question, "Will I outlive my money?"

- Also, **fewer people have a pension coming**. Today, it is just teachers, firemen, police officers, and some government employees in-line for a pension. That equates to only about 13% of the labor force versus a much higher percentage several decades ago when the US was a more unionized, manufacturing economy.

- And looking down the road, **social security alone will simply not provide enough** to live the life you are used to, and very long term, **its viability is in doubt** due to mismanagement and demographics.

- We are also **paying more of our healthcare costs out-of-pocket today.**

- In general, **the financial world is becoming increasingly complex** and competitive. Even though there are many professionals available to help, you need a fair amount of basic knowledge to even understand their language and to be able to make good decisions, and protect yourself, if you choose to work with them.

Why Save? Money Grows!

I have already stated several times that money can grow, here I will explain how this happens. We are talking about why we *need* to save and why we *should* start saving young. We have many future financial needs, and it is increasingly our responsibility to fund those needs. Perhaps the most important reason to save is that **money set aside can be put to work and grow.**

Money can grow because of the power of compounding. Einstein called compounding interest the eighth wonder of the world. Save, then let the mathematical magic of compounding interest take care of your future.

Here is an example of compounding:

- For mathematical simplicity, assume an annual investment return of 10%.

- In one year, $1000 grows into $1100 ($1000 X 1.10 = $1100).

- What about year 2?

- Your original $1000 grows again.

- Remarkably, so does the $100 you earned in year 1!

- **Your interest earns interest. Your money makes more money!**
- ...even while you sleep or play.

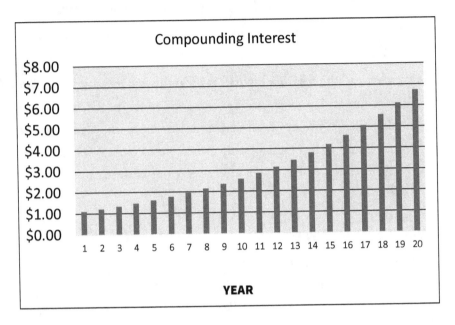

I encourage you to look closely at the above chart to visualize the power of compounding interest. The amount of money you have is not just growing, it is accelerating. $1 doubled to $2 in about seven years, and that doubles again in about 14 years. A bit farther out than my chart shows and your $1 would be $8, that's life changing growth. I used a 10% rate of return here for mathematical simplicity. That rate of return surely can't be guaranteed in the real world. It is possible to earn 10% over the long term, with money invested in stocks, but even 5, 6, or 7% delivers enough growth to get excited about compounding.

Hopefully, seeing the power of money's growth potential will motivate you to want to live a lifestyle focused on saving. **Saving money is the first step to building wealth. Compounding drives the growth that builds wealth.**

Not only are we seeing that money can grow, we are starting to understand the math that drives growth. Now, let's elaborate on an earlier activity. Recall, our opening activity was to consider two people who saved for a decade, but one saved in their 20s and one in their 40s.

Here we expand and consider four people, to cover more ages:

- Again, they each save $100/month for 10 years. Then they stop.
- Person one saves in their 20s, then stops. Person two in their 30s. Person three in their 40s. Person four gets a late start and saves in his/her 50s.
- For all of them, the $1,200 they save each year is invested and grows at 7% per year until age 60.

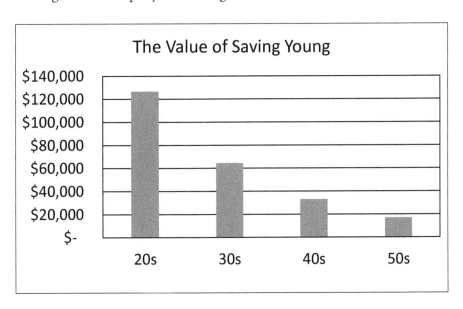

The above chart shows the power of starting early. The person that saved in their 20s builds wealth and accumulates over $125,000 by age 60. The person that saved the $12,000 in their 50s only sees it grow to about $16,000.

This illustration should hammer home, hopefully emphatically, the power of compounding and the benefit of starting at a young age. The younger you start saving, the more years your money has to work for you; however, **it's never too late to save for your future.**

You NEED Money to Compound!

It is exciting to think of money working *for* you, compounding and growing! Perhaps this excitement offsets some of the dread you experience when you have to list all of your future financial needs. **But you must understand a critical point: you actually NEED the compounding.** Unless you have unique earning power (or win the lottery), your future financial needs will likely exceed what you can save and set aside. So again, you need your money to grow, and the earlier you start saving and compounding, the more it can grow. Saving earlier is also good because growth is rarely in a straight line. There will be periodic losses. The earlier you start means more time to ride out and recover from fluctuations in returns. If you start too late you may find yourself in retirement with a nest egg too small to both support withdrawals and recover from market declines.

You also need compounding growth due to inflation. The term inflation refers to a general rise in prices of a *broad basket* of goods. In the US, we generally don't see inflation extremes other countries experience. On average, our prices tend to increase about 2-3% a year. Thus, the purchasing power of a dollar today is diminishing over time. We need some growth simply to maintain the same purchasing power going forward.

INSIGHT - THE *RULE OF 72*

The *rule of 72* is a quick and easy **formula to estimate the number of years required to double your money**. The value of the rule is that you can do the math in your head.

How does it work? Take the number 72 and divide it by the annual interest rate assumption. The result is the number of years required to double your money.

For example, growing at 7% per year, money can double in about 10 years (72/7= about 10). Start saving in your 20s and you may get an extra doubling compared to someone who starts saving later. Think of that, an extra doubling; now that is money working *for* you. **Start saving young because the math is in your favor and it is good to form the behavioral habits early in life.**

$X saved by age 30 can = about 2X by 40, 4X by 50, 8X by 60!

INSIGHT - THE *RULE OF 72* FROM AN INFLATION PERSPECTIVE

I just described the *rule of 72* as a means to estimate the number of years it takes for money to double. **We can also use this rule from an inflation perspective and see how many years it takes for your purchasing power to fall in half.** Assume inflation is 2.5% per year, which is fairly typical when the economy is doing well. Take 72 and divide it by 2.5, and you get about 29 (round to 30 for simplicity). **This means that with 2.5% inflation, a dollar today will lose half its purchasing power in about 30 years.** Or said another way, you'll need $2 in the future to buy what $1 buys today. You might say 30 years in the future is too long to care about. But when you are in your 20s or 30s, 30 years in the future is your investment horizon and years until retirement. So, it matters! We need growth!

ACTIVITY - BEGIN TO UNDERSTAND YOUR FINANCIAL SITUATION & SAVING GOALS

A critical mantra we will repeat throughout this section is that you should understand your financial situation. *You can't control what you don't understand.* **An initial exercise is to deeply consider and write down estimates for your future financial needs, the reasons you need to save.**

- What are your **infrequent bills**? e.g. insurance, property taxes, etc.

- Do you have an **emergency fund** to cover several months of basic expenses?

- Do you have high interest **debt that should be a priority to pay off *early***?

- Can you list additional **saving priorities over various time horizons**?

  - **Short-term** - Vacation plans, required home/car maintenance, etc.

  - **Medium-term** – New car, house down payment, wedding(s), etc.

  - **Long-term** – College funds, retirement, etc.

Next - I move from teaching *why* we must save, to devoting two chapters covering *how* **to save!**

CHAPTER ELEVEN

HOW TO SAVE (*YOU* CONTROL YOUR MINDSET)

Chapter fit in overall framework:

Problem	Solution	Epiphany
Soaring college debt	Get a career, not just a degree, with minimal debt	A *broken* system
		Career goals - Pursue your passions
		Estimate your earning potential
		Choose a school you can afford
Career uncertainty	Proactively stay employable	Career uncertainty *will* affect you
		Adopt a mindset that embraces change
		Keep investing in yourself
Lack of financial literacy	Learn **why** we *must* save	You *need* compounding
	Learn **how** to save	*You* control your mindset
		Save *first*
		Live for *today* - "What's your butter?"
	Learn **what** to do with savings	It's *not* too intimidating

At *no* time in my life did I believe I had *any* chance of becoming a major league baseball player. Don't get me wrong, I love the game, and I could throw very hard *for a 12-year-old*. But I am skinny (actually wiry sounds more athletic) and, since I was born blind in one eye, I have no depth perception. But, did I mention I love the game? If only I had more control over the dream of playing professionally.

This chapter will begin a discussion on how to save money by focusing on a *mindset* to succeed. Specifically, I will answer two important questions:

1. Why is mindset critical?

2. Why make mindset my starting point in teaching how to save?

CHAPTER EPIPHANY – YOU CONTROL YOUR MINDSET

You are more in control of your life and possible outcomes than you might think. You can *choose* a mindset and lifestyle of daily choices to save money. You can choose to put yourself in a position to begin to build wealth.

Why is Mindset Critical?

With the mindset to adopt a lifestyle of making daily choices to save money, you can set out to achieve your financial goals. What is so powerful is that **YOU control your mindset**. Saying "you control your mindset" to save money sounds obvious. But I encourage you to see just how powerful your mindset is here in this financial context. Having a mindset to succeed is powerful but doesn't always get the results you want. For example:

- **You can't just choose to be a professional athlete.** You might want it really badly. Unlike me, you might even be that rare talent that has a chance, and you work really hard. But you can't just choose to get called up to the majors.

- Or **you can't just choose to get a 1600 on the SAT Math and English sections**. It would be an incredible accomplishment and surely help your college applications, freeing you up to focus on the essays. Many people study hard to improve their scores. But again, you can't just choose to get a 1600.

- **Yet, you *can* choose a mindset, attitude, and lifestyle to save money.**

You are more in control of your life and finances than you think! I'm not promising the world here. I'm not saying everyone can will themselves to become millionaires. What I am saying is, trust me, you have more control than you might realize. **You can control daily decisions about discretionary spending**. Ask yourself: Do I need all of the $4 coffees? Do I need all of the $10 lunches and $100 nights out at restaurants? You choose what kind of car you drive. You choose the college to attend. You can choose not to be house poor (i.e., in a house you know you can't afford). You can choose the amount and kind of stuff that fills that house, garage, shed, or the rented storage unit. The sooner we all ingrain this mindset into our daily lives, the better, because then we may never get into financial troubles that might otherwise plague us.

Why Make Mindset My Starting Point?

Let's move on to my second question, "Why make mindset my starting point?" The **answer is two-fold. The right mindset can serve as both an *initial spark* and be there to ensure *sustained* success.** Realizing you are more in control than you thought with respect to your ability to choose a lifestyle of daily decisions to save money can be **the initial spark motivating you**:

- **To want to learn more** about personal finance.
- **To *see* money differently,** for example, as a tool or means to an end and not an end in itself. Recall the many bankrupt celebrities and professional athletes. Just having a large pile of money wasn't enough for them because of the daily decisions and lifestyle choices they made. They brought home $10 million a year but somehow spent $12 million.
- **To change your *relationship* with money.** Rather than just working for money, I teach how to put your money to work for you.

In addition to an initial spark, **the proper mindset is also what you need to drive the daily decisions necessary to ensure *sustained, lifelong success.***

Mindset goes hand in hand with discipline, and creating personal wealth is rooted in personal discipline. The reality is, much of this personal finance material is easy to understand, and you may already know some or all of it. But can you stick with it? Can you routinely defer today for the future?

Testing whether or not people could defer today for tomorrow was the subject of a famous experiment in the 1960s. Stanford University researchers offered children one marshmallow, but if they waited, they got two. Follow-up studies a full 20 and even 30 years later found that, in aggregate, the children who had delayed gratification had better life outcomes: better careers, higher incomes and even more stable family situations. **Saving money is forgoing spending or experiencing something today, for tomorrow. Saving money is your *daily* marshmallow experiment.**

Next - We go from purely a mindset to specific methods. I will teach **the nuts and bolts of *how* to save.**

CHAPTER TWELVE

How to Save (Save *First* & Live for *Today*)

Chapter fit in overall framework:

Problem	Solution	Epiphany
Soaring college debt	Get a career, not just a degree, with minimal debt	A *broken* system
		Career goals - Pursue your passions
		Estimate your earning potential
		Choose a school you can afford
Career uncertainty	Proactively stay employable	Career uncertainty *will* affect you
		Adopt a mindset that embraces change
		Keep investing in yourself
Lack of financial literacy	Learn **why** we *must* save	You *need* compounding
	Learn **how** to save	*You* control your mindset
		Save *first*
		Live for *today* - "What's your butter?"
	Learn **what** to do with savings	It's *not* too intimidating

Pilots use checklists. Engineers use procedures. Chefs use recipes. What do savers use? **Is there a sustainable, repeatable process for saving money?** Can there be a process for saving money that is not painful or tedious?

I am promoting financial literacy by teaching *why* we save, *how* to save and *what* to do with savings. **This chapter will continue, and complete, a discussion on *how* to save.** The last chapter covered adopting a mindset to make daily decisions to save money. This chapter dives into the mechanics of saving.

CHAPTER EPIPHANY #1 – SAVE FIRST

I will outline a disarmingly simple approach to saving money: *save first*, which means pay yourself first, and then live off what remains.

CHAPTER EPIPHANY #2 – LIVE FOR TODAY

Save and spend wisely. Live a disciplined life saving for the future, but don't forget to live for today. I will describe a technique that allows you to reward yourself with a particular *want* that feels more like a *need*.

Save First

This is where the rubber meets the road. Sadly, this is where teachers of financial literacy can lose people. We can lose students' interest, not because it gets too complicated, but if we allow it to get too tedious. Very few of us want to live by a detailed budget. That is why **my approach is not built around a detailed budget. Instead, my approach is built around a lifestyle choice to save, and as you will see, the rest begins to take care of itself.**

The figure below illustrates a *typical or traditional* approach to saving money; the formula is **Income minus Expenses equals Savings.**

Income - Expenses = Savings

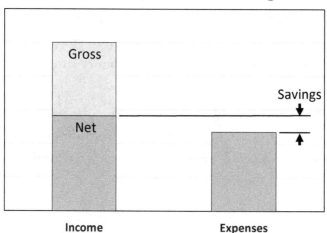

This traditional approach is an intuitive, but I believe flawed, framework. The plan here is to try to spend less money than you bring home. What is left over is your savings. **However, in this approach, savings are an afterthought and often don't happen because they are not a priority.** *(See the **Supplements section** at the back of the book for a **Topical Discussion on Understanding Taxes** to explain tax brackets and deriving net pay).*

This figure rearranges the above formula and illustrates **the approach I advocate, a technique called** *save first*; Income minus Savings equals Expenses.

Income - Savings = Expenses

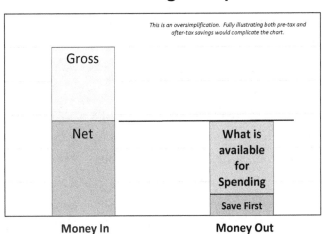

Literally save first then live off what remains. When I read about this in my 20s, I had an epiphany – an aha moment, truly a life changing event for me. I hope it is for you too. Here, savings are planned and set-aside *upfront*. You pay yourself first.

Save First Savings Goals

"Save first then live off what remains" is obviously easier said than done. It **takes daily effort and is built on discipline and setting clearly defined saving goals.** Vague goals like *saving for a good retirement* won't inspire you into action. Quantified and focused goals are easier to dedicate real energy to achieving.

Having savings goals across multiple time horizons enables you to see the rewards when near-term goals are achieved so that you do not give up on long-term goals where there is no instant gratification.

Save First Strategies

Here are some specific strategies that others have used successfully to *save first*. You can:

- **Save 10% of your pay[8].** This idea comes from one of the oldest books on personal finance, *The Richest Man in Babylon*. In this 1926 classic by George Clason, the reader learns how to save from tradesmen, herders, and merchants as they talk to the richest man in Babylon, since he had previously been very poor himself. His guidance offers common sense financial advice through parables, revealing how to create, grow, and preserve wealth. He specifically teaches how to get more out of what you earn, how to avoid debt, and how to put your money to work for you in ways that manage your risk to safeguard your savings. At the heart of his approach is that when you get paid 10 *coins* you immediately put one aside, put it to work, and then live off what remains. The book highlights stories of how people implemented this strategy, at first doubting it or even scoffing at it but then realizing it is possible to follow.

- **Use the 50/30/20 Rule.** Some people use guidelines, such as a rough 50/30/20 split, to allocate their spending between *needs/*

wants/savings. I have found this more useful as a reality check looking back on recent actual numbers.

- **'Trick' yourself into saving.** In the first strategy above, immediately saving 10% of your income, then living off what remains, is the equivalent of structuring your life around an income that is fictitiously 10% less; this is typically doable. A more extreme version of this strategy is **in a two-income house, save one salary and live off the other**. My wife and I did this before we had kids, so I can attest to its plausibility.

Live for Today! What's Your Butter?

This section provides some much-needed perspective to ensure that you still live your life for today versus being 100% focused on deferring spending for the future.

We have covered the mindset needed for sustained success at making daily decisions to save, why we save and why we need to start saving young. As part of how to save, **I don't want you to forget to live your life today.**

When I think of giving people advice to *live for today*, while still saving and preparing for the future, **I think of the expression "What's your butter?"** Let me explain. I'm honestly not sure if this is a memory or a story that I heard, it is about a woman speaking at church. She openly discussed surviving at or below the poverty line. Yet, regardless of how she had to make sacrifices, she bought real butter. If you don't know, real butter costs much more than margarine. She said she *had* to. She needed it to bake the way she wanted for her grandchildren, to feel whole as a loving grandmother.

I encourage you to think about *"What's your butter?"* **What is the discretionary expense category you actually need to live your life today in a rewarding way? What is one *want* that feels more like a need?**

Live within your means but also live your life today. For my family, our butter is travel and we make choices to do that. We live in an unassuming 1970s house, drive used cars with a combined 300,000 miles on them, don't eat out much, and the kids worked very hard to earn scholarships, but we like the family experience of travel. We've made some great memories traveling together. We know we are fortunate because travel is more expensive than even the best butter. The key is sticking with the personal process to maintain a lifestyle built around saving.

Take a Few Steps Back to Discuss the Language of Saving

There is simply no way to avoid the fact that a lifestyle of making daily decisions to save and build wealth takes effort. To help with this effort, we need to briefly **get into the weeds of my disarmingly simple approach to saving money.** Let's take a few steps back to ensure we are all on the same wavelength. Let's go over some terminology, so we have **a common language about saving money. This language is critical to understand your financial situation. You can't control what you don't understand.**

$$\text{Income} - \text{Expenses} = \text{Savings}$$
$$\downarrow$$
$$\text{Income} - \text{Savings} = \text{Expenses}$$
$$\downarrow$$
$$\text{Income} - \text{Savings} = \textit{Needs} + \textit{Wants}$$
$$\downarrow$$
$$\text{Income} - \text{Savings} - \textit{Needs} = \textit{Wants}$$

Let's walk through the above graphic from top to bottom:

- **Line 1** – (Income - Expenses = Savings) is the flawed approach I led off with.

- **Line 2** – Rearrange, (Income - Savings = Expenses) is the better approach, the *save first* approach. This requires you to know your saving priorities and have clear saving goals over multiple time horizons. Pre-tax savings, *off-the-top* before you bring home money, *force* saving for long-term needs. I can't emphasize enough how I encourage pre-tax savings. Additional savings can target paying debt off early or other savings goals over all time horizons.

- **Line 3** – Acknowledges that expenses are split between *needs* and *wants*.

- **Line 4 – The bottom line (literally) – Rearranging one last time we solve for *Wants*.** Save first, meet your true *needs* then spend what is left on some *wants*.

Briefly, Getting More Specific - Detailed Expense *Buckets*:

Understanding your spending is best done by tracking expenses. To do this right, we need to get a bit more specific with expense categories and language than the simple split between *needs* and *wants*:

- <u>Fixed expenses</u> – Fixed expenses are those that are the same each month like mortgage, rent, cable, etc.

- <u>Variable expenses</u> – Variable expenses are also periodic bills, but they vary based on usage, for example, electricity and water utilities. What you will find is that while they tend to vary month to month, they are surprisingly similar year to year.

- <u>Discretionary</u> - Discretionary expenses are mostly *wants*: entertainment (e.g. attending a movie or concert), activities (e.g. golfing, skiing), eating out, buying gifts, etc. You can dial back, or even do without, expenses in this bucket.

- <u>Infrequent (annual / semi-annual / lumpy / out of your control)</u> – Infrequent expenses such as home and auto insurance or local school taxes are best thought of or computed on a monthly basis so that you set the money aside and have it ready when needed (i.e., once or twice a year). Other expenses in this bucket may be large but lumpy (i.e., irregular in size and timing); lumpy expenses can be major home or car maintenance that are somewhat predictable but also partly out of your control.

To summarize the previous discussion, **it is critical to understand your financial situation.** If you have a pre-tax savings option available to you through an employer, I urge you to fully participate. Then, understand what your take home pay is after paying taxes and deductions such as for Social Security and Medicare. Take home pay is your starting point for additional savings through expense control. To control spending, you will find that even *needs* can be fine-tuned, that is, reduced. And some *wants* can and must be done without. **The amount you can spend after**

meeting your savings goals and *needs,* is an important number to know. You can literally keep track and countdown from that number during any given month or between paychecks. While you can **think of my savings approach as** *save first,* you can **remember my spending approach as** ***what's left*** - w*hat's left* after meeting your savings goals and needs.

Illustrating *Save First* and Spend *What's Left*

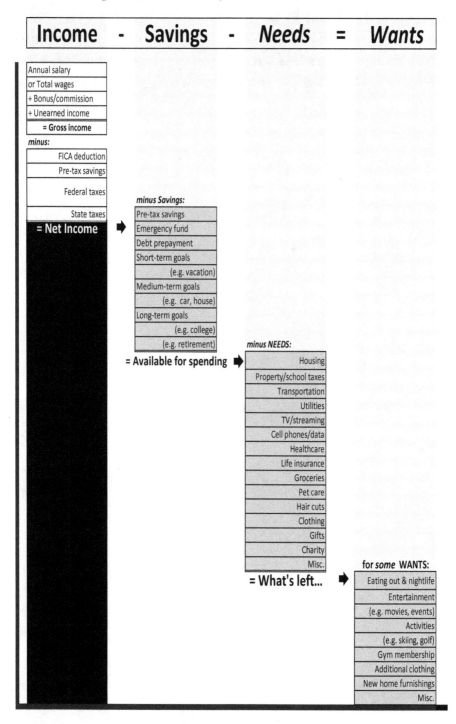

Income	-	Savings	-	Needs	=	Wants

Annual salary
or Total wages
+ Bonus/commission
+ Unearned income
= Gross income
minus:

FICA deduction
Pre-tax savings
Federal taxes
State taxes

= **Net Income**

minus Savings:

Pre-tax savings
Emergency fund
Debt prepayment
Short-term goals
(e.g. vacation)
Medium-term goals
(e.g. car, house)
Long-term goals
(e.g. college)
(e.g. retirement)

= **Available for spending**

minus NEEDS:

Housing
Property/school taxes
Transportation
Utilities
TV/streaming
Cell phones/data
Healthcare
Life insurance
Groceries
Pet care
Hair cuts
Clothing
Gifts
Charity
Misc.

= **What's left...**

for *some* WANTS:

Eating out & nightlife
Entertainment
(e.g. movies, events)
Activities
(e.g. skiing, golf)
Gym membership
Additional clothing
New home furnishings
Misc.

INSIGHT - A FORMULA FOR SUCCESS?

INCOME – SAVINGS – NEEDS = WANTS

Is the formula I recommend for saving and spending a *guarantee* for success? Unfortunately, no. Algebraically, the disarmingly simple formula is most likely to lead to success if you have high income, clear savings goals, and low spending habits. Obviously, the stars won't align like that for everyone.

- **Even very high income is no guarantee of success:** We already saw how even high income, but with no personal process or discipline to save first or control spending, can result in failure to save and even bankruptcy.

- **Lean spending habits are no guarantee of success:** Tight control on spending alone is not a recipe for guaranteed success because income may be low, the cost-of-living in the location you reside could be prohibitively high, or savings goals are not clear or the top priority.

- **There is really only one guarantee:** The scenario that comes closest to a guarantee is if you have a very *low* income, **then the formula *won't* work**! The reality is that a very low income, e.g. household income at $30,000 or less, may not even cover your Needs, let alone discretionary Wants. With that said, I have seen low income households still participate in employer-offered pre-tax savings plans, to at least receive their employer's matching contribution, and accumulate a sizeable sum over many years due to compounding. But even then, meeting day-to-day Needs can be a challenge and Wants are a rare luxury.

- **Review your Needs:** Growing income and cutting spending help you save. Another area of opportunity is to review and *right-size* your true Needs!

Step-By-Step Procedure to *Save First* and Spend *What's Left*

Everyone's situation is different but by using our common language you can create a personal tracking system. See the Your Sherpa, LLC website (www.**your**financial**sherpa**.com) for a spreadsheet template. While it is never too late to start, it is ideal if you start early in life and ingrain good habits when young.

Next - We need to grow what we saved, and build wealth. The next chapter delves into **what you can do with your savings**.

CHAPTER THIRTEEN

WHAT TO DO WITH SAVINGS
(IT'S *NOT* TOO INTIMIDATING)

Chapter fit in overall framework:

Problem	Solution	Epiphany
Soaring college debt	Get a career, not just a degree, with minimal debt	A *broken* system
		Career goals - Pursue your passions
		Estimate your earning potential
		Choose a school you can afford
Career uncertainty	Proactively stay employable	Career uncertainty *will* affect you
		Adopt a mindset that embraces change
		Keep investing in yourself
Lack of financial literacy	Learn **why** we *must* save	You *need* compounding
	Learn **how** to save	*You* control your mindset
		Save *first*
		Live for *today* - "What's your butter?"
	Learn **what** to do with savings	It's *not* too intimidating

You saved! Now what?

Don't be "like a deer in the headlights." We all know the expression. It refers to being caught in a state of paralysis. Sometimes people aren't totally frozen, yet they still aren't accomplishing what they need to do. Have you ever watched a hockey team on a power play obsessively passing the puck, looking for the perfect opportunity, but never shooting? Well, you can't score if you don't shoot. In golf, even if your putt is perfectly online, you can't sink it if you don't hit it hard enough. You get the idea.

This chapter will provide a high-level overview of what to do with your savings. This chapter will provide enough for you to make an initial move!

CHAPTER EPIPHANY: WHAT TO DO WITH SAVINGS? IT'S NOT TOO INTIMIDATING

Part III is entitled *Daily Decisions to Save and Build Wealth*. My concern that too few people are saving motivated me into action. Now that we know how to save, it is time to talk about growing savings and building wealth. Now it is time to talk about what to do with savings. Here, I show you that **understanding some language and the landscape of savings and investments is enough to decide how to move ahead**: managing your investments yourself, engaging professionals, or a combination of the two. **What to do with your savings? Really, it is *not* too intimidating to move forward.**

You Saved! Now What?

Disclaimer – What I Do NOT Do

I need to start with a *disclaimer*. As you'd suspect, a discussion on *what to do with savings* gets into investing. Recall, however, investing is NOT my focus. My focus is on saving money, setting some aside for the future. My initial concern, and what motivated me to teach financial literacy, was my observation that too few people are saving money, and you have to save before you can invest.

To be clear, I am not a money manager, registered investment advisor, or financial planner. There is an army of them out there wanting to help you, if and when you decide to work with them. I actually did work as a senior analyst and portfolio manager in the research department of a large institutional money manager for almost 20 years. I was part of a team responsible for investing and managing billions of dollars of other people's money. I have an MBA in finance, and I am a Chartered Financial Analyst. Despite this prior experience, providing specific investment advice is not what I do in this book or at Your Sherpa, LLC.

What I Do

What I *will* do is **provide an overview of your options, introduce the language, and describe the general landscape** associated with savings and investing decisions. This is an important part of being financially literate. You will be ready if and when you decide to put your savings to work.

Savings versus Investments - Think Protection versus Growth

Perhaps the best starting point is ensuring that we all understand that **savings and investments are actually different**. Savings is the money you set aside for the future. Investing is more about putting your savings to work, to grow. Importantly, not all savings should be invested.

Think, protection versus growth. Some savings are really in effect spent money: money saved and earmarked for a very near-term need. In this case, you can't put this money at risk because you don't have time to recover from losses, if they occur. For this money, depositing in a bank is appropriate. It will be safe, in fact most deposits in the bank are insured. The bank will pay you a small amount of interest as they use your money to support loans to other bank customers. This type of lending and borrowing helps other people get home mortgages or small business loans and propels the broader economy through what academics call a multiplier effect.

Investing, on the other hand, is more about seeking growth and really putting your money to work for you. **Investing applies to longer time horizons in which you want to leverage compounding. Investing entails more risk** but over the long run you should be compensated with more reward: a higher return than you would achieve in a savings account. Since growth is not predictable, will not occur in a straight line, and you can lose money at any time, investing is not appropriate for money needed in the short-term.

Investing is a very broad topic, you could pursue a full degree program in finance or have a whole career in the investment field. Again, I will keep it at an overview level and touch on some important terminology and concepts that will help you prepare to make savings and investing decisions.

Investment Decisions and Considerations - Allocation

Allocation refers to your overall investment mix of cash, bonds, stocks, real estate, etc. An appropriate mix is **largely determined by your age** (i.e., years until retirement) as this indicates your ability to ride through possible down periods in returns. Also, **a key factor determining your mix is your personal risk tolerance,** discussed below. When I was a professional stock picker, I frequently had people ask me for my thoughts on individual stocks. I believe most people fail to realize that the broader allocation decision, the mix of their assets, is likely a more important decision to determine their overall returns. The allocation decision, deciding on your mix of assets, should be a higher priority and is a better use of limited time than being focused on the stock of an individual company.

Investment Decisions and Considerations - Diversification

Diversification refers to mitigating risk, the risk that an investment may lose value or underperform other investments on a relative basis. Diversification is about spreading out your risk, not concentrating your risk in too few investments. You have likely heard the expression *don't put all your eggs in one basket.* Diversification is a form of risk management just in case one of your baskets spills and breaks those eggs. If that happens, you want other eggs that remained safe. If one of your investment decisions performs poorly, or even becomes worthless, you want a diverse set of other investments to potentially pick up the slack.

Investment Decisions and Considerations - Risk Tolerance

Risk tolerance refers to your personal ability to assume risk. Another expression you have likely heard is *risk versus reward.* Owning individual stocks or the whole stock market has more risk associated with it than holding a bank account or a bond, but over time they tend to reward you with higher returns. It is very difficult to predict the stock market direction over a short time period, but over the long-term the market should increase to at least reflect the long-term growth trajectory of corporate earnings plus dividends. At times, individual company fundamentals and even macroeconomic conditions can take jaw dropping declines. **Risk tolerance is a personal and qualitative metric. It may be best illustrated by simply considering your ability to sleep at night knowing your investments.** People feel more pain associated with losses than joy associated with gains. So, when you consider risk versus reward, you need to have a sense of how you will feel, cope, and behave in turbulent times.

Investment Decisions and Considerations - More Risk Management

We mentioned that **diversification is a form of investment *risk management*. But risk management isn't limited to investments.** We employ risk management in our everyday lives; **think of insurance.** There are many types of insurance: life, home, auto, and umbrella. The concept of insurance is basically that for a rather small or nominal amount, a premium, you pass the risk of a major loss onto another party (i.e., the insurance company). This major loss may be statistically unlikely but the magnitude, if it occurred, could be devastating, both as a disruption to your life and to your finances.

Another form of risk management may be the measures you take to protect your identity. Or even simply the common sense employed on a daily basis (e.g. knowing not to access personal bank information on a public wi-fi!).

INVESTING INSIGHT – CRITICAL MASS

Critical mass is a term used in several contexts. Generally, it means to reach a critical point of being sustained (e.g. a sustainable reaction in the context of nuclear fission or sustainable growth in the context of a new business venture). In the context of saving and investing, you can think of critical mass as the *ultimate objective*.

Reaching critical mass means you have successfully saved and built wealth to the point that your nest egg is large enough to generate income sufficient to live off. That is, you live your life and spend investment income, but your nest egg doesn't shrink.

If you recall, in the dedication of this book I referenced Bob Brinker. Bob Brinker's investment process inspired many people to work towards, what he called, *The Land of Critical Mass™*. Few people reach investment critical mass but working towards it inspires a lifestyle of daily decisions to save and build wealth.

Next - I recap Part III. Note, for more details on *what to do with savings*, **see the Supplements** at the end of the book.

CHAPTER FOURTEEN

Part III Recap

Part III fit in overall framework:

Problem	Solution	Epiphany
Soaring college debt	Get a career, not just a degree, with minimal debt	A *broken* system
		Career goals - Pursue your passions
		Estimate your earning potential
		Choose a school you can afford
Career uncertainty	Proactively stay employable	Career uncertainty *will* affect you
		Adopt a mindset that embraces change
		Keep investing in yourself
Lack of financial literacy	Learn **why** we *must* save	You *need* compounding
	Learn **how** to save	*You* control your mindset
		Save *first*
		Live for *today* - "What's your butter?"
	Learn **what** to do with savings	It's *not* too intimidating

Part III set out to teach people to be financially literate. Four chapters aimed at delivering life-changing epiphanies on **why we must save, how to save, and what to do with savings.** We reviewed a harsh reality that you are increasingly responsible to fund your financial future. To do it right, you must start early and maintain determination and discipline. After completing Part III, you are better equipped **to make daily decisions to save and build wealth**.

Part III covered a lot of ground teaching financial literacy. Let's recap why we save, how to save, and what to do with savings.

Why we _must_ save: We have to save because we have many **future financial needs** over various time horizons. We also must save because it is **increasingly our responsibility** to fund our own financial futures since we are living longer, fewer of us are due to receive a pension, and we are paying more for our healthcare. Importantly, we also must save because **money can be put to work and can grow!** Unfortunately, even if you understand your money can grow, unless you have tremendous earning power, you simply can't set enough aside for future needs. **Thus, you NEED your money to grow!** It is not just a bonus that your money can make more money due to compounding interest. It is not a luxury or gimmick. It is a necessity. Since you _need_ growth, you should be saving as early in life as possible so that the money has more time to compound.

How to save: **We led off with mindset.** Having the right mindset is critical to setting and achieving financial goals. The reason mindset is so critical is because **_you_ control your mindset**. You can choose a lifestyle of daily decisions that save money. A mindset change can be a catalyst and **_initial_ spark** that gets you interested in saving and approaching money differently. Also, a mindset to remain disciplined and to routinely make wise spending choices is what is **needed for _sustained_ lifelong success**.

The best approach to saving money is to **_save first!_** Yes, **save first then live off what remains**. Saving first and living off what remains is easier said than done, but with clear saving goals over short, medium, and long-term time horizons, you can set out to do it.

Since saving is forgoing today for tomorrow, I don't want you to forget to live for today. Make daily decisions to save, but also live for today. Identify your _butter_ even as you save for future priorities.

Part III included some specific suggestions on how to **understand and track what you spend**.

Live by the formula...

Income - Savings - *Needs* = *Wants*

And finally, in Part III, we discussed _what_ to do with savings: To reiterate, my focus is on teaching people to save money, not invest money. You have to save before you can invest. What motivated me is my observation that too few people are saving money in the first place. I provided **an overview** of what you will need to understand as you consider investing options. Perhaps you do it yourself. Perhaps you enlist a professional. Either way, you will need **to understand the language and landscape of managing savings and investing to build wealth, and doing so is NOT as intimidating as some people think**. I provided a broad overview of the **language and landscape** including:

- **Saving versus investing** - Savings being more about protection and investments being more about growth.

- **Allocation** - The mix of your assets between cash, stocks, bonds, etc.

- **Diversification** - Not having all of your eggs in one basket.

- **Risk tolerance** - Your ability to mentally and emotionally handle losses or the ups and downs of financial markets. Your ability to sleep at night when you think of your investments.

- **Insurance** – The act of transferring large risks to another party for a nominal fee or premium.

You did it! You learned how to avoid the obstacles (i.e., debt and job uncertainty) that prevent people from being in a position to save. Then you learned why we must save, how to save, and what to do with savings.

Next Steps:

- Set or realign your mindset to make daily decisions to save.
- Set out to understand your financial situation.
- Plan and prioritize your savings goals, and track and control your spending.

Congratulations!

CONCLUSION - SUMMARY

Here is a summary of the entire book. If I led off with this, you may not have read anymore. **I hope you had at least one epiphany moment!**

Summary:

I teach financial literacy to students and young adults, engaging parents in the process. My focus is on helping people save money and build wealth.

What motivated me into action? I believe there is a potential, virtuous cycle in life – if you achieve your financial goals, you can take more control of your path forward, and having more control of your life increases the chances of unlocking and realizing your personal potential. Yet, surveys show approximately 40% of Americans can't raise even $400 for an emergency and about 78% continue to live paycheck to paycheck, even if their income increases. People simply aren't saving money.

As I see it, there are **three problems** preventing people, particularly young people, from setting out to achieve financial goals, and thus initiating the virtuous cycle we just spoke of:

1. **Soaring college debt** – You can't even begin to save if you have too much college debt.

2. **Career uncertainty** – You can't save if you can't get and hold a good job, particularly a job in which you can grow your income.

3. **A general lack of financial literacy** – Even if people are in a position to save, that is they don't have excessive college debt and do have a good job, they do not know how to make daily decisions to save money and build wealth.

My mission is to provide you with **a road map** to help you combat these three problems; *personal solutions to set you up for success.*

My **solution to soaring college debt** is to show you how to attain your career goals with minimal debt. First, we must define the problem. The college selection process is a broken system characterized by a self-perpetuating cycle driving and supporting ever higher costs. The conditions driving this self-perpetuating cycle are: 1. college is expensive, 2. loans are often required but loans are exceedingly easy to obtain, 3. the players in the system do not emphasize the negatives associated with debt nor discourage debt, 4. adding fuel to the fire, in the end students and families often make purely emotional decisions (i.e., falling in love with a campus or school name) and choose a school they really can't afford, and 5. schools are enabled by these factors to further raise prices (schools know that those who can afford the full price will pay it and others will get loans). Schools also overinvest in stadiums, amenities, and administrators and further raise the price to earn a return on that investment; perpetuating the cycle. My specific solution is to:

- **Pursue your passions**. While I want you to get a degree with minimal debt, the real objective and top priority is a job and career! Deeply consider your career goals. Ask, what are your passions, interests, skills, talents, gifts? What would you *love* to do? Is college even right for you? Do you need college to achieve your career goals? Remember that in the end, your future success likely rests more with you than the school you choose.

- **Understand your potential earning power**. Estimate your future income potential associated with your career goals. You pay off debt with your future earnings. Avoid a debt load you *can't possibly* pay back.

- **Choose a school you can afford.** An affordable school **requires a debt level you can payoff, which is approximately 1x your estimated starting salary**. The key is to take the emotion out of the college selection decision. Start by only looking at schools you can truly afford. Also, parents and students need to talk openly about finances early in the process. Students should know how much the family has saved for college. My recommended strategy for paying for college is to try to avoid loans by parents and minimize loans to students. College is expensive. We can't change that fact. Yet, it is your responsibility to make sound financial decisions that are best for you in the long run.

My **solution to career uncertainty** is to teach how to proactively stay employable. First, we must define the problem. Career uncertainty is due to changing technology, globalization, limited wage growth, a skills gap, demographics, and other factors. My specific solution is to:

- **Adopt a mindset that embraces change**. Adopt a realistic perspective. Realize *nobody owes you a career*. Staying employed is your responsibility. Own your career like it is a sole proprietorship. Your business is you. Keep yourself marketable and flexible. Position and protect your business to benefit in a changing world because no one else will for you.

- **Keep investing in yourself.** This entails learning on the job and in life, outside of and beyond school. Demonstrate to others a constant desire to learn. Be proactive, expecting to change jobs or even careers. Expect to have to be your own advocate, your own brand manager. Craft, and be able to articulate to others, your message – describing your passions and skills. Understand your degree is not the be all and end all. Keep developing skills in line with your interests and even push the limits of your comfort zone. Know that soft skills (e.g., listening, communicating, decision making, leadership) are critical for advancement.

Finally, my **solution to the general lack of financial literacy** is to teach people *why* we must save, *how* to save, and *what* to do with savings. Important concepts are:

- **You *need* compounding.** Why must we save? We need to save money because we have so many future needs and life events, and it is increasingly our responsibility to support ourselves. We also save because money can grow due to the power of compounding interest. What many people don't realize is that we *need* compounding; you need money to grow because we typically can't set aside enough for all future needs. Save young to give compounding more time!

- ***You* control your mindset.** Mindset is critical because you control your mindset. You can literally choose a lifestyle of making daily decisions to save.

- **Save *First*.** How do you save? Is there a better approach or method than others? I advocate, "Save First", then live off what remains. It really is possible, even life changing, if you are disciplined and have clear savings goals. Follow the formula ***Income – Savings – Needs = Wants***. Save first, meet your true needs, and spend what is left on *some* wants.

- **Live for *Today*.** Save and build wealth for the future by saving first, but don't forget to live today. Everyone has a want they really need. Treating yourself helps you feel whole and propels you on for sustained financial success.

- **What do you do with your savings? Make a move.** Don't be a deer in the headlights. Don't be too intimidated to put some of your savings to work, to grow; that is how you build wealth. Understand key investing terms and concepts such as *savings versus investing* (think protection vs. growth), *allocation* (think asset mix), and *diversification* (think risk management by not having all of your eggs in one basket).

I am excited for you and confident that the time you devoted here will pay dividends. Now go out and put these lessons into practice. Change some behavior. Develop good habits. Ensure you stay in a position to save and then **make daily decisions to save and build wealth**. See www. yourfinancialsherpa.com for additional resources and to see how to follow me for updates.

SUPPLEMENTS
(*OPTIONAL*, TOPICAL READING)

Topical Discussion 1 – Understanding Taxes

To fully understand how your gross pay is reduced to become your net (or take home) pay, you must understand taxes.

The **federal tax code is called a marginal tax bracket system,** meaning it refers to the **tax rate on your *marginal* (next or last) dollar** of income. If you earn a high income and are in the highest bracket, you don't pay the highest rate on *all* of your money earned. The higher your income, the higher the tax bracket you extend into, but you pay the same rate as everyone else in lower brackets. See examples below, which use 2018 tax rates:

tax rate	tax bracket
10%	$0-$9,525
12%	$9,526-$38,700
22%	$38,701-$82,500
24%	$82,501-$157,500
32%	$157,501-$200,000
35%	$200,001-$500,000
37%	$500,001+

Example 1: $55,000 per year salary		
tax rate	tax bracket	tax owed
10%	$0-$9,525	$953
12%	$9,525-$38,699	$3.501
22%	$38,700-$55,000	$3.586
24%		
32%		
35%		
37%		
	total Fed taxes owed	$ 8.039
	effective rate	15%

Example 2: $550,000 per year salary		
tax rate	tax bracket	tax owed
10%	$0-$9,524	$953
12%	$9,525-$38,699	$3.501
22%	$38,700-$82,499	$9.636
24%	$82,500-$157,499	$18.000
32%	$157,500-$199,999	$13.600
35%	$200,000-$499,999	$105.000
37%	$500,000-$550,000	$18.500
	total Fed taxes owed	$ 169.190
	effective rate	31%

Once you have computed the taxes owed in each bracket, you can add up your total taxes owed. If you divide that by your gross pay, it gives you one single percentage and that is what people refer to as **the *effective* tax rate.**

Topical Discussion 2 – Credit versus Debit

I am often asked for my opinion on what is best, using a credit card or debit card. In general, spending can be with cash, a check, a debit card, a credit card, or person-to-person (P2P) (e.g. Venmo). Some broader trends in overall spending provide a good starting point to enter the credit versus debit debate:

- Cash use is waning. Some people see cash as inconvenient to carry and it can't be used for online purchases.
- Checks are being replaced by online banking (e.g. bill payment features).
- P2P is relatively new, growing very fast, and still evolving.
- Credit and debit card use is growing globally. In fact, growth has been fairly steady for years, at an elevated rate of around 10% per year.

There are pros and cons associated with both debit and credit card use:

- Debit card pros – Convenient and enforces discipline (i.e., you must have the money in your account to make a purchase).
- Debit card cons – Few. Purchases don't help you build a credit score.
- Credit card pros – Convenient, good for online purchases, earn rewards (e.g. travel miles), and payments go towards building a credit score.
- Credit card cons – Potentially significant! Very high interest rate if you don't pay off your balance each month. Also, you run the risk of overspending money you do not have. Credit card use requires discipline.

In summary, the self-regulating feature of debit cards is very powerful: you can't spend what you don't have. Regarding credit card use, with discipline, they are good as you get rewards and build a credit history. Importantly, you should not let an unpaid credit card balance build from month to month. Extreme or unforeseen circumstances like a major car or home repair may result in a balance. After such an occurrence it should become a high priority to pay off that debt. Maintaining a rolling monthly balance and paying high interest rates should not be the norm.

Topical Discussion 3 – Credit Score

Here, I define and discuss a **credit score**.

A **credit score** is part of a **credit report** compiled by a **credit bureau**. Banks and other lenders use the score **to gauge your credit worthiness**; should they lend to you and trust that you will pay them back? For example, a bank may use your credit score in determining whether they should give you a mortgage to buy a home. A consumer lender may use the score to determine if they should give you an auto loan.

A credit score is computed from your payment history and the length of your credit history. Definitely pay your bills on time as late payments become bad data in your credit report and score.

You can check your credit score for free three times per year, once at each of the three credit bureaus:

www.experian.com

www.transunion.com

www.equifax.com

Your report will explain the numerical score, which has a range from 400 to 900. Become familiar with what is in your personal report. Know that you can dispute and have corrected inaccurate data or outdated data (e.g. data on a credit card you have in fact closed or a loan you have already paid off). You may be surprised to realize that by following your reports and correcting errors you will likely improve your score and improve your ability to get future loans or obtain more attractive borrowing rates.

Topical Discussion 4 - Rent or Buy?

This topical summary provides perspective on the decision to rent or buy the place where you live. Here is some *general guidance* on this major life decision:

- **First and foremost, don't willingly become *house poor*: don't buy a house you can't afford!** There are specific calculations you can do to determine if your house payment as a percentage of income crosses a dangerous threshold. However, I am referring more to your own judgement. If the payment would leave you noticeably short on cash for the rest of your financial obligations, or force you to routinely sacrifice in other areas, then it is likely a house you can't afford. If the payment would prevent you from building an emergency fund or saving for life events, then, again, it is likely a house you can't afford.

- Renting *pros*: Renting is flexible and good for a short time, or if you aren't sure how long you will live in an area.

- Renting *cons*: When you rent, the payment is *gone* (i.e., spent as opposed to *invested*); you are not building equity in something you will someday own. Only the owner benefits in the appreciation of the value when they sell.

- In my opinion, it is probably best, and a good conservative approach, to view a home as a roof over your head and not as an investment. Don't financially stretch into a home that is difficult to pay for on a monthly basis because you think that when you ultimately sell it you will make a big profit. If the value does go up, see that as a bonus but don't expect it or need it.

- If / when you do buy, plan for a down payment of at least 10%, as this is typical and a minimum requirement for many mortgages. A down payment of 20% allows you to avoid a cost each month called PMI insurance.

- Know that home prices vary significantly by area - *location, location, location.*

- Monthly mortgage payments depend on the interest rate at which you borrowed to buy the home. I recommend a fixed rate for certainty versus a variable rate.

- Owning a home means you pay the mortgage + insurance + taxes. Taxes can add up...property + school + garbage pick-up + misc. These total costs are called the carrying costs of owning a home.

Topical Discussion 5 – Some Additional Investment Terms

Liquid versus Illiquid: I already indicated that when you consider savings versus investing to think in terms of protection versus growth. Other terminology to segregate assets is to say *liquid* versus *illiquid* funds. Liquid accounts allow easy access to your money. Examples include cash, bank accounts, short-term CDs, and money market savings accounts. In contrast, illiquid accounts cannot be converted to cash easily or quickly. For example, pre-tax retirement investment accounts penalize early withdrawals and physical assets like a home may take time to sell and you may need the proceeds for your next purchase.

Pre-tax versus After-tax: Another way to separate accounts is to distinguish between pre-tax or after-tax.

A pre-tax account is an investment account in which the money goes in *before* it has been taxed (i.e., 'off the top'). This type of investment account is typically available through an employer (referred to as a 401k if offered by for-profit companies or a 403b offered by tax-exempt organizations). People who are self-employed can set them up too. There are big tax benefits associated with pre-tax accounts, and I recommend you take full advantage of them. Some employers *match* all or part of your contribution; that is free money! These accounts are typically for long-term investments (e.g. college and retirement). They are great ways to *force* saving for long term needs. Reinforcing the fact that these accounts are for the long term, there are penalties for early withdrawal. So, while the money goes in pre-tax, and hopefully grows each year without being subject to tax, eventually withdrawals will be subject to tax. This often works out well because in retirement you are likely in a lower tax bracket than in your peak earning years.

An after-tax account is funded with after-tax money: money that has already been taxed, producing your take-home pay. An after-tax account is money you saved in addition to pre-tax savings. This money can be deposited in a savings account for short-term needs or invested for intermediate or longer-term needs. Money that is invested should have a long enough time horizon to seek growth and allow for ups and downs in investment values. A Roth IRA is a specific type of after-tax investing account in which investment gains are not taxed in the future.

That concludes the supplemental topical summaries. I hope they were helpful.

WORKS CITED

1. Goldy-Brown, S. (July 28, 2018). *The Average Cost of College in 2018.* Student Debt Relief. https://www.studentdebtrelief.us/news/average-cost-of-college-2018/

2. (2015). *The death of the American pension: Shifting the retirement burden from employers to workers has created an enormous financial crisis.* My Budget 360. http://www.mybudget360.com/pension-death-percent-of-americans-with-a-pension-defined-benefit-contribution/

3. Board of Governors of the Federal Reserve System. (May 2018). *Report on the Economic Well-Being of U.S. Households in 2017.* https://www.federalreserve.gov/publications/files/2017-report-economic-well-being-us-households-201805.pdf

4. CareerBuilder. (August 2017). *Living Paycheck to Paycheck is a Way of Life for Majority of U.S. Workers.* http://press.careerbuilder.com/2017-08-24-Living-Paycheck-to-Paycheck-is-a-Way-of-Life-for-Majority-of-U-S-Workers-According-to-New-CareerBuilder-Survey

5. Center for Microeconomic Data. (November 2018). *Quarterly Report on Household Debt and Credit.* https://www.newyorkfed.org/medialibrary/interactives/householdcredit/data/pdf/hhdc_2018q3.pdf

6. Grove, A. (1996). *Only The Paranoid Survive – How to Exploit the Crisis Points that Challenge Every Company and Career.* New York, NY: Doubleday.

7. Gladwell, M. (2008). *Outliers: The Story of Success.* US: Little, Brown and Company.

8. Clason, G. (1926). *The Richest Man in Babylon.* New York, NY: Penguin Books.

ACKNOWLEDGMENTS

A quick thank you to the key people who inspired the content in this book:

- My wife and kids for the examples they set in pursuing one's passions.

- My nieces and nephews for being sounding boards.

- Paul Celuch and others at College Assistance Plus for genuinely caring about students and families and providing insights on getting the degree you need with minimal debt.

- Ebrahim Busheri of Manning & Napier Advisors for his thoughts on EQ and soft skills.

- Dr. Ernesto Sirolli who created Enterprise Facilitation™ to engage passionate, aspiring entrepreneurs and unlock the potential within them.

- Andy Grove of Intel for opening my eyes and serving as my call to action, through his book.

ABOUT THE AUTHOR

Who am I? Do I understand your perspective?

For a combined 33 years, I was an engineer, a senior analyst, and a portfolio manager. I have an MBA in finance and earned the Chartered Financial Analyst (CFA) designation. I've been trained to be an analytical problem solver, and I have provided training after I created an internal school to teach new hires. I have lots of experience in finance and managing money. As a professional investor I was quite literally paid to study the world around me with a critical eye, to identify and call out problems, and to seek out potential solutions. That is how college debt, career uncertainty, and the general lack of financial literacy got on my radar.

I see your perspective because I have lived it:

- **With respect to college debt:** As a parent I have gone through the college search, application, attendance, and payment process. I am borderline enraged at the cost to attend most schools, the rate of increase, the lack of justification for that cost, the lack of price transparency, the underlying assumption that everyone should go, and worried, genuinely worried, about the amount of debt some students and families are assuming to pursue degrees.

- **With respect to career uncertainty:** I have worked in industries that experienced disruptive change. I have had my specific job function disappear overnight. I have had to repeatedly and proactively reinvent myself just to survive, to keep my job.

- **With respect to financial literacy:** Early in life, the math of how money can compound and grow caught my attention. I adopted a lifestyle making daily decisions to save. Eventually I switched careers and as an analyst was part of a team responsible for managing other people's money, a huge responsibility which made me respect that hard-earned sliver of savings even more. I am a parent too, so I have faced, and continue to face, the opportunities and challenges to teach my own kids how to handle money and make daily decisions to save.

- **And now with Your Sherpa, LLC:** I teach others about saving money and building wealth and how to overcome or avoid obstacles to saving, such as college debt. I work with students and young adults, engaging parents in the process.

CPSIA information can be obtained
at www.ICGtesting.com
Printed in the USA
LVHW081702100220
646431LV00006B/793